CCC

Course on Computer Concepts

Sample Papers For Exam Success

By

BPB Editorial Board

FIRST EDITION 2020

ISBN: 978-93-89845-242

LIMITS OF LIABILITY AND DISCLAIMER OF WARRANTY

The information contained in this book is true to correct and the best of author's & publisher's knowledge. The author has made every effort to ensure the accuracy of these publications, but cannot be held responsible for any loss or damage arising from any information in this book.

All trademarks referred to in the book are acknowledged as properties of their respective owners.

NIELIT is in no way connected with this book. This book is written solely for the benefit and guidance of students appearing for NIELIT examination.

Distributors:

BPB PUBLICATIONS
20, Ansari Road, Darya Ganj
New Delhi-110002
Ph: 23254990/23254991

DECCAN AGENCIES
4-3-329, Bank Street,
Hyderabad-500195
Ph: 24756967/24756400

MICRO MEDIA
Shop No. 5, Mahendra Chambers,
150 DN Rd. Next to Capital Cinema,
V.T. (C.S.T.) Station, MUMBAI-400 001
Ph: 22078296/22078297

BPB BOOK CENTRE
376 Old Lajpat Rai Market,
Delhi-110006
Ph: 23861747

Published by Manish Jain for BPB Publications, 20 Ansari Road, Darya Ganj, New Delhi-110002 and Printed by him at Repro India Ltd, Mumbai

Preface

With the recent revision of the syllabus, the NIELIT has changed the exam pattern. All this has been kept in mind while writing this book. The book in your hand is strictly based on the NIELIT Latest Syllabus of Year 2019 and promises to deliver the content keeping in mind the learning outcomes of the subject.

Errata

We take immense pride in our work at **BPB Publications** and follow best practices to ensure the accuracy of our content to provide with an indulging reading experience to our subscribers. Our readers are our mirrors, and we use their inputs to reflect and improve upon human errors if any, occurred during the publishing processes involved. To let us maintain the quality and help us reach out to any readers who might be having difficulties due to any unforeseen errors, please write to us at:

errata@bpbonline.com

Your support, suggestions and feedbacks are highly appreciated by the BPB Publications' Family.

Table of Contents

Model Test Paper I

1. **भीम एप के द्वारा 1 दिन में कितना पेमेंट किया जा सकता है?**
   (a) ₹10000 (b) ₹2000
   (c) ₹5000 (d) ₹100000
2. **Impress में अधिकतम Zoom कितना होता है?**
   (a) 3000% (b) 30%
   (c) 50% (d) 400%
3. **WWW के लिए पहला ग्राफिकल Web Browser कौन सा है?**
   (a) गूगल क्रोम (b) मोजाईक
   (c) इंटरनेट एक्प्लोरर (d) मोज़िला फायरफॉक्स
4. **LibreOffice Writer में कॉपी करने का शॉर्टकट क्या होता है?**
   (a) Ctrl+Shift + C (b) Alt + C
   (c) Ctrl + C (d) Ctrl+A+C
5. **B2B का पूरा नाम क्या होता है?**
   (a) Base to Base (b) Business to Business
   (c) Base to Business (d) None of these
6. **Libre Office Impress में मास्टर स्लाइड फंक्शन किस मेन्यू मे मिलता है?**
   (a) स्लाइड (b) स्लाइड शो
   (c) फॉरमैट टूल्स (d) टूल्स
7. **प्रेषक को वापस लौट आने वाला मेल क्या कहलाता है?**
   (a) बाउंसड मेल (b) बैक मेल
   (c) रिटर्न मेल (d) स्पैम मेल
8. **किस प्रकार की टोपोलॉजी में सूचना का प्रवाह एक दिशा में होता है?**
   (a) स्टार (b) बस
   (c) मेश (d) रिंग
9. **Calc में कितने रो और कॉलम होते है?**
   (a) 1024 और 1048576 (b) 1048576 और 1024
   (c) 1048578 और 16385 (d) 16385 और 1048578
10. **HTML का पूरा नाम क्या होता है?**
    (a) हाइपर टेक्स्ट मार्कअप लैंग्वेज
    (b) हाइपर टेक्स्ट वेब लैंग्वेज
    (c) हाइपर टेक्स्ट वेबसाइट लैंग्वेज
    (d) हाइपर टेक्स्ट वेब डिजाइन लैंग्वज
11. **एप्लीकेशन लेयर कौन सी सेवा प्रदान करती है?**
    (a) End to End (b) Process to Process
    (c) Both of the above (d) None of the above
12. **इंटीग्रेटेड चिप का विकास किस ने किया था?**
    (a) सी.वी. रमन (b) रोबर्ट नायक
    (c) आइंस्टाइन (d) जे.एस. किल्बी
13. **ई-मेल निम्न में से किस का उदाहरण है?**
    (a) इंस्टेंट मेकिंग (b) इंस्टेंट मैंसेजिंग
    (c) इंटरनल मैसेजिंग (d) मेलिंग
14. **एस. बी. आई का पूरा रूप क्या होता है?**
    (a) सुपर बैंक ऑफ इंडिया (b) स्टेट बैंक ऑफ इंडिया
    (c) भारतीय स्टेट इनकम (d) स्टेट बैंक इंडोनेशिया
15. **किस पीढ़ी के कम्प्यूटर आकार में सबसे बड़े होते थे?**
    (a) प्रथम पीढ़ी (b) द्वितीय पीढ़ी
    (c) तृतीय पीढ़ी (d) चतुर्थ पीढ़ी
16. **IMEI नंबर देखने के लिए किस कोड का प्रयोग करते हैं?**
    (a) *60# (b) *#06#
    (c) $#6# (d) #16#
17. **एटीएम और क्रेडिट कार्ड में CVV कितने डिजिट का होता है?**
    (a) 5 अंक (b) 4 अंक
    (c) 3 अंक (d) 3 अंक
18. **निम्नलिखित में से कौन सी एक्सटेंशन लिब्रा ऑफिस से संबंधित नही है?**
    (a) .odt (b) .ods
    (c) .rtf (d) .odp
19. **लिब्रा ऑफिस में प्रेजेन्टेशन क्या है?**
    (a) Impress (b) Calc
    (c) Writer (d) None
20. **लिब्रा ऑफिस इंप्रेस में Zoom का न्यूनतम साइज क्या होता है?**
    (a) 10% (b) 5%
    (c) 3000% (d) 200%
21. **Umang App में N का क्या अर्थ है?**
    (a) National (b) New Age
    (c) New (d) None of the above
22. **लिब्रा ऑफिस Calc में फाइल एक्सटेंशन क्या है?**
    (a) .ods (b) .doc
    (c) .xlx (d) .odp
23. **MICR का पूरा नाम क्या है?**

(a) मैग्नेटिक इंक कैरेक्टर रिकग्निशन
(b) मैग्नेटिक इंक कैरेक्टर रीडर
(c) मैग्नेटिक इंक केर रिकग्निशन
(d) मैग्नेटिक इंक केग रीडर

24. सबसे छोटा कम्प्यूटर है?
(a) मिनी कम्प्यूटर (b) सुपर कम्प्यूटर
(c) माइक्रो कम्प्यूटर (d) मेनफ्रेम कम्प्यूटर

25. QR कोड का अर्थ होता है?
(a) Quick Recorder Code
(b) Quick Response Code
(c) Quick Register Code
(d) None of the above

26. POS का पूरा नाम क्या होता है?
(a) Point of Sale (b) Power on Switch
(c) Part of Sale (d) None of the above

27. यूपीआई किसके द्वारा develop किया गया?
(a) स्टेट बैंक ऑफ इंडिया
(b) नेशनल पेमेंट कॉरपोरेशन ऑफ इंडिया
(c) इंडियन पेमेंट गेटवे
(d) रिजर्व बैंक ऑफ इंडिया

28. क्या डाइल करने से यूएसएसडी सेवाओं का लाभ उठाया जा सकता है?
(a) *121# (b) 11#
(c) *123# (d) 111रु

29. असेम्बलर कौन सा सॉफ्टवेयर है?
(a) एप्लीकेशन सॉफ्टवेयर (b) सिस्टम सॉफ्टवेयर
(c) ऊपर के दोनों (d) उपरोक्त में से कोई नहीं

30. Calc में A1+A2 को ऐड करने से क्या परिणाम आएगा?
(a) 0 (b) ###
(c) 1 (d) उपरोक्त में से कोई नहीं

31. वैक्यूम ट्यूब तकनीक कौन सी पीढ़ी में प्रयोग की जाती थी?
(a) पहली पीढ़ी (b) दूसरी पीढ़ी
(c) तीसरी पीढ़ी (d) चौथी पीढ़ी

32. AEPS में E का पूर्ण रूप क्या है?
(a) Electronic (b) Electric
(c) Enabled (d) None of the above

33. Umang App में कितनी भाषाओं का प्रयोग किया जाता है?
(a) 10 (b) 13
(c) 12 (d) 6

34. लिब्रा ऑफिस में Calc में अधिकतम कॉलम का नाम है?
(a) XFD (b) AMJ
(c) AJS (d) उपरोक्त में से कोई नहीं

35. .Com किससे संबंधित है?
(a) Commerce (b) Commercial
(c) Organization (d) None

36. पहले सर्च इंजन कौन सा है?
(a) Archie (b) Yahoo
(c) Google (d) None of the above

37. पॉवर पॉइंट में Show Preview करने के लिए क्या Select करेंगे?
(a) Slide Show (b) Home tab
(c) Design (d) उपरोक्त सभी

38. IPV6 का पता कितने Bit का होता है?
(a) 32 (b) 64
(c) 28 (d) 128

39. Libreoffice Calc and Excel डेट और टाईम की शॉर्टकट की क्या होती है?
(a) Ctrl+; (b) Ctrl+Shift+:
(c) Both (a) and (b) (d) None of the above

40. Twitter में Twit करते समय अधिकतम कितने कैरेक्टर प्रयोग कर सकते हैं?
(a) 180 (b) 140
(c) 280 (d) 150

41. LAN का पूरा नाम क्या है?
(a) लोकल एरिया नेटवर्क
(b) लॉजिकल एरिया नेटवर्क
(c) लोकल एरिया नेट
(d) उपरोक्त में से कोई नहीं

42. ₹200000 से ₹500000 के बीच ट्रांसफर करने पर कितना चार्ज लगता है?
(a) 15 (b) 25
(c) 5 (d) 20

43. Umang का अर्थ क्या है?
(a) Unified Mobile Application for New-age Governance
(b) Unified Mobile Application for News Governance
(c) Unified Mobile Application for Network Governance
(d) None of the above

44. Phone Pay क्या है?
(a) मैसेंजर (b) सोशल साईट

(c) ई वॉलेट (d) ऐप्लीकेशन

45. IDS का पूरा नाम क्या है?
(a) Intrusion Direction System
(b) Intrusion Detection System
(c) Intrusion Detection Source
(d) None of the above

46. Full Form of ECB?
(a) Extra Commercial Borrow
(b) External Commercial Borrowings
(c) External Computer Borrowings
(d) None of the above

47. Full Form of NUUP?
(a) National Unified Uniq Platform
(b) National Unified USSD Platform
(c) Network Unified USSD Platform
(d) None of the above

48. Full Form of WIFI?
(a) Wireless Facility (b) Wireless Fidelity
(c) Wireless File (d) Wired Fidelity

49. एक्सेल फार्मूला बार में अगर फार्मूला से पहले = लगा हो तो क्या आएगा?
(a) #name
(b) #name?
(c) फॉर्मूला बार में जो भी लिखा होगा वही
(d) ###

50. इनमें से मोबाईल ऑपरेटिंग सिस्टम है?
(a) एंड्राइड (b) विंडो फोन
(c) BADA (d) उपरोक्त सभी

51. RTGS के द्वारा न्यूनतम ट्रांसफर की लिमिट है?
(a) 100000 (b) 300000
(c) 200000 (d) न्यूनतम कोई सीमा नहीं

52. इनमें से कौन सा आउटपुट डिवाइस नहीं है?
(a) मॉनिटर (b) प्लॉटर
(c) लाइट पेन (d) प्रिंटर

53. वेब पेज किस फॉर्मेट में सेव होता है?
(a) एचटीएम (b) एचटीएमएल
(c) दोनों (d) वेब

54. mod(50,-7) का क्या मान होगा?
(a) 6 (b) -6
(c) -1 (d) 1

55. Full Form of IMEI?
(a) International Mobile Equipment Identity
(b) Internet Mobile Equipment Identity
(c) International Mobile E Ideitity
(d) None of the above

56. Toggle key का उदाहरण है?
(a) स्क्रॉल लॉक (b) कैप्स लॉक
(c) Insert (d) उपरोक्त सभी

57. फॉयरफॉक्स (Firefox) क्या है?
(a) ऑपरेटिंग सिस्टम (b) वेब ब्राउजिंग
(c) सर्च इंजिन (d) सोशल नेटवर्किंग साइट

58. ABRS Stand for....
(a) Aadhaar Based Remittance Service
(b) Aadhaar Board Remittance Service
(c) Advanced Based Remittance Service
(d) None of the above

59. `Calc में अधिकतम वर्कशीट कितनी होती हैं?
(a) 1000 (b) 10000
(c) 5000 (d) 255

60. =product(5,2) का मान क्या होगा?
(a) 3 (b) 10
(c) 1 (d) 7

61. Full Form of UTR?
(a) Unique Transaction Reference
(b) Unlimited Transaction Reference
(c) Unique Transfer Reference
(d) Unique Transaction Row

62. Full Form of EBCDIC?
(a) Extended Binary Coded Decimal Interchange Code
(b) Extended Bit Coded Decimal Interchange Code
(c) Extended Binary Code Decimal Interchange Code
(d) Extended Binary Coded Dot Interchange Code

63. Full Form of NEFT?
(a) National Electronic Fund Transfer
(b) National Electric Fund Transfer
(c) National Electronic Formula Transfer
(d) National Electronic Fund Transit

64. लिब्रा ऑफिस सॉफ्टवेयर पैकेज में कई एप्लीकेशन सॉफ्टवेयर शामिल हैं?
(a) True (b) False

65. (B2C) बिजनेस To कंज़्यूमर का मतलब व्यापारी ग्राहक को वस्तएं भेजता है?
(a) True (b) False

66. BADA मोबाइल ऑपरेटिंग सिस्टम है?
(a) True (b) False

67. लाइनेक्स ओपन सोर्स ऑपरेटिंग है?
(a) True (b) False

68. Internet or www अलग अलग हैं?
(a) True (b) False

69. विंडो एक ऑपरेटिंग सिस्टम है?
(a) True (b) False

70. सीपीयू में ALU अंकगणित व तार्किक संचालन का कार्य करता है?
(a) True (b) False

71. JPG फाइल फॉर्मेट इमेज के लिए होता है?
(a) True (b) False

72. कॉलम को जोड़ने का कौन सा फॉर्मूला सही है?
(a) =sum(B1:B1048576)
(b) =sum(B1,B1048576)
(c) =add(B1:B1048576)
(d) None of the above

73. Cloud Computing क्या है?
(a) अपने डाटा को इंटरनेट पर सुरक्षित करना
(b) कम्प्यूटर को इंटरनेट से जोड़ना
(c) डाटा को कम्प्यूटर में सेव करना
(d) All of the above

74. Libre Office Row की कुल संख्या है?
(a) 1048576 (b) 1047857
(c) 10678 (d) 1024

75. ट्विटर में # का क्या यूज होता है?
(a) किसी विषय पर चर्चा करना
(b) किसी को टैग करना
(c) किसी को मैसेज भेजना
(d) उपरोक्त सभी

76. क्रेडिट कार्ड में APR क्या है?
(a) Interest Rate
(b) Annual Percentage Rage
(c) Both of the above
(d) None of the above

77. Umang का पूर्ण रूप क्या है?
(a) Unified Mobile Application for New-age Governance
(b) Unifier Mobile Application for New-age Governance
(c) Universal Mobile Application for New-age Governance
(d) None of the above

78. इनमें से कौन सा सबसे अच्छा विश्वकोष (encyclopedia) है?
(a) Wikipedia (b) Google
(c) Quora (d) Yahoo

79. DES का का पूर्ण रूप क्या है?
(a) Data Encryption Slot
(b) Data Encryption Standard
(c) Data Encryption Solution
(d) None of the above

80. हेडिंग 3 के लिए शॉर्टकट की है?
(a) Ctrl+3 (b) Shift+3
(c) Shift+1 (d) Ctrl+1

81. ऐनालॉग और डिजिटल कम्प्यूटर का मिक्स रूप है?
(a) Super Computer (b) Hybrid Computer
(c) Personal Computer (d) None of the above

82. पहले स्लाइड पर जाने की शॉर्टकट की क्या है?
(a) Pageup (b) PageDown
(c) Home (d) End

83. Blockchain टेक्नालॉजी क्या है?
(a) बिटकॉयन में इस्तेमाल होने वाली टेक्नालॉजी है
(b) सुरक्षित लेन-देन में सहायक
(c) Both of the above
(d) None of the above

84. डिस्क्रिप्शन और एंक्रिप्शन का प्रदर्शन क्या है?
(a) यह हमारे डाटा को सुरक्षित रखता है
(b) सुरक्षित लेन-देन में सहायक
(c) दोनों
(d) कोई नहीं

85. फेसबुक में अधिकतम कितने फ्रेंड्स हो सकते हैं?
(a) 1000 (b) 5000
(c) 256 (d) No limit

86. बैंक को इंटरनेट से कब अटैच किया गया?
(a) 1994 (b) 1995
(c) 1996 (d) 2000

87. CPU में कौन सी स्टोरेज डिवाइस लगी होती है?
(a) ट्रांजिस्टर (b) कैश मेमोरी
(c) हार्ड डिस्क (d) All of the above

88. NEFT की टाइमिंग क्या है?
(a) 8.00 am to 6.00 am (b) 8.00 am to 7.00 am
(c) 6.30 am to 5.30 am (d) None of the above

89. Calc का फाइल एक्सटेंशन?

(a) .odc (b) .odt
(c) .ods (d) .odp

90. TCP/IP में कितने लेयर होते हैं?

(a) 7 (b) 4
(c) 5 (d) 3

91. FTP में F का मतलब क्या है?

(a) File (b) Font
(c) Format (d) Function

92. IPV6 Address Bits.... ?

(a) 28 (b) 128
(c) 32 (d) 64

93. इंस्टाग्राम के फाउंडर कौन है?

(a) Kevin Systrom and Mike Krieger
(b) Marc Zuckerberg
(c) Bill Gates
(d) None of the above

94. Mac Address Size?

(a) 12 digits (b) 6 byte
(c) 48 bits (d) All of the above

95. फंक्शन के अंदर फंक्शन को क्या कहते है?

(a) Function (b) Nested Function
(c) General Function (d) Condition Function

96. Full Form of set..... ?

(a) Secure Electronic Transactions
(b) Security Electronic Transactions
(c) Security end Technology
(d) None of the above

97. निम्नलिखित में से कौन सा वेब ब्राउज़र है?

(a) याहू (b) गूगल
(c) मोज़िला फायरफॉक्स (d) यूट्यूब

98. File नेम और Extension के बीच क्या लगाकर अलग करते हैं?

(a) @ (b) .(dot)
(c) $ (d) #

99. क्रेडिट करना किससे संबंधित है?

(a) बैंक में पैसे जमा करना (b) कैश निकालना
(c) Dabit-Credit (d) None of these

100. CC क्या दर्शाता है?

(a) Cancel Copy (b) Create Copy
(c) Carbon Copy (d) None of the above

Answers

1.	(a)	2.	(a)	3.	(b)	4.	(c)
5.	(b)	6.	(a)	7.	(a)	8.	(a)
9.	(b)	10.	(b)	11.	(a)	12.	(a)
13.	(b)	14.	(b)	15.	(a)	16.	(b)
17.	(d)	18.	(c)	19.	(a)	20.	(b)
21.	(b)	22.	(a)	23.	(a)	24.	(c)
25.	(b)	26.	(a)	27.	(b)	28.	(a)
29.	(b)	30.	(a)	31.	(a)	32.	(c)
33.	(b)	34.	(b)	35.	(b)	36.	(a)
37.	(a)	38.	(d)	39.	(c)	40.	(c)
41.	(a)	42.	(b)	43.	(a)	44.	(c)
45.	(b)	46.	(b)	47.	(b)	48.	(b)
49.	(c)	50.	(d)	51.	(c)	52.	(c)
53.	(c)	54.	(b)	55.	(a)	56.	(d)
57.	(b)	58.	(a)	59.	(b)	60.	(b)
61	(a)	62	(a)	63.	(a)	64.	(a)
65.	(a)	66.	(a)	67.	(a)	68.	(b)
69.	(a)	70.	(a)	71.	(a)	72.	(a)
73.	(a)	74.	(a)	75.	(a)	76.	(c)
77.	(a)	78.	(a)	79.	(b)	80.	(a)
81.	(b)	82.	(c)	83.	(c)	84.	(c)
85.	(b)	86.	(c)	87.	(d)	88.	(b)
89.	(c)	90.	(b)	91.	(b)	92.	(b)
93.	(a)	94.	(d)	95.	(b)	96.	(a)
97.	(c)	98.	(b)	99.	(a)	100.	(c)

Model Test Paper II

1. **Writer में Ctrl+Y से क्या होता है?**
   (a) Undo किया गया टेक्स्ट Redo करना
   (b) Redo किया गया टेक्स्ट Undo करना
   (c) Both (a) and (b)
   (d) None of the above

2. **Umang App में N का पूर्ण अर्थ बताइए?**
   (a) National (b) New
   (c) New-age (d) None of the above

3. **एनालिटिकल इंजन का आविष्कार किसने किया?**
   (a) Charles's Baggage (b) John Napier
   (c) Libnitz (d) None of the above

4. **बिंग का आविष्कार किसने किया?**
   (a) एप्पल (b) गूगल
   (c) माइक्रोसॉफ्ट (d) All of these

5. **वेब पेज को प्रिंट करने के लिए किस शॉर्टकट कुंजी का इस्तेमाल किया जाएगा?**
   (a) Ctrl+P (b) Ctrl+Shift+12
   (c) Both of the above (d) None of the above

6. **By default फाइल से होती है?**
   (a) डॉक्यूमेंट (b) डेस्कटॉप
   (c) डाउनलोड (d) इनमें से कोई नहीं

7. **Save as करने की शॉर्टकट कुंजी क्या होती है?**
   (a) F12 (b) Ctrl+S
   (c) Ctrl+F12 (d) Shift+F12

8. **कम्प्यूटर बंद होने पर किसमें डाटा सेव रहता है?**
   (a) Volatile (b) Non-Volatile
   (c) Both (d) None of the above

9. **आधार कार्ड में कुल नंबर कितने होते है?**
   (a) 10 (b) 11
   (c) 12 (d) 13

10. **प्रस्तुतीकरन में नई स्लाइड डालने की शॉर्टकट कुंजी क्या होती है?**
    (a) Ctrl+M (b) Ctrl+N
    (c) Alt+N (d) Alt+N

11. **B1 से B5 तक की रेंज हैं?**
    (a) B1*B5 (b) B1&B5
    (c) B1#B5 (d) B1:B5

12. **प्रस्तुतीकरन में ऐड कर सकते हैं?**
    (a) पिक्चर को, मूवी को नहीं
    (b) मूवी को लेकिन पिक्चर को नहीं
    (c) मूवी तथा पिक्चर दोनों को
    (d) उपरोक्त में से कोई नहीं

13. **Writer में न्यूनतम Zoom साइज कितना होता है?**
    (a) 5% (b) 10%
    (c) 20% (d) 30%

14. **इंस्टाग्राम के फाउंडर कौन हैं?**
    (a) Konstantin Guericke
    (b) Kevin Systrom
    (c) Jawed Karim
    (d) None of the above

15. **FTP में F का मतलब क्या है?**
    (a) For (b) File
    (c) Folder (d) All of these

16. **BHIM App के द्वारा एक दिन में Pay लिमिट कितनी होती है?**
    (a) 20000 (b) 10000
    (c) 1000 (d) कोई सीमा नहीं

17. **If we want to add some document in mail then we choose:**
    (a) Compost (b) Add
    (c) Attachment (d) Link

18. **Outlook में कितने MB का अटैचमेंट किया जा सकता है?**
    (a) 20 (b) 25
    (c) 40 (d) 35

19. **WIFI का पासवर्ड मिनिमम कितने अंकों का होता है?**
    (a) 7 (b) 10
    (c) 8 (d) 9

20. **QR Code का प्रयोग कहाँ करते हैं?**
    (a) एजुकेशन में (b) मार्केटिंग में
    (c) ऊपर के दोनों (d) इनमें से कोई नहीं

21. **Libreoffice में Ruler की Shortcut key होती हैं?**
    (a) Alt+Shift+C (b) Ctrl+R
    (c) Ctrl+Shift+R (d) Window+L+R

22. **वेब पेज को प्रिंट कर सकते हैं?**
    (a) True (b) False

23. **क्या हम एक पीसी पर दो ऑपरेटिंग सिस्टम यूज कर सकते हैं?**

(a) True (b) False

24. क्या जानवरों के नाम का पासवर्ड रखना चाहिए?
(a) True (b) False

25. सफारी एक सर्च इंजन है?
(a) True (b) False

26. DOS GUI पर आधारित है?
(a) True (b) False

27. UPI NCPI द्वारा स्थापित है?
(a) True (b) False

28. लिब्रे ऑफिस एप्लीकेशन सॉफ्टवेयर नहीं है?
(a) True (b) False

29. Full Form of APR in Credit Card?
(a) Annual Percentage Rage
(b) All Percentage Rage
(c) Annual Percent Rage
(d) Annual Percentage Range

30. File Extension name of Calc?
(a) .ods (b) .odt
(c) .xls (d) .wps

31. MAC is written in - hexadecimal?
(a) True (b) False

32. ASCII is of how many bits?
(a) 8 bits (b) 16 bits
(c) 32 bits (d) 64 bits

33. NABAARD किसी सिफारिश पर स्थापित हुआ?
(a) B. Sivaraman Committee, 12 July 1982
(b) B. Sivaraman Committee, 11 July 1988
(c) B. Sivaraman Committee, 10 July 1982
(d) B. Sivaraman Committee, 9 July 1982

34. To Show company logo on each slide which slide should be edited?
(a) Master Slide (b) Slite
(c) Logo Slide (d) New Slide

35. सी.पी.यू. के पास कौन सी मेमोरी होती है?
(a) कैश मेमोरी
(b) Main Memory
(c) Primary Memory
(d) Secondary Memory

36. एक फोल्डर को डायरेक्टरी भी कहते हैं?
(a) True (b) False

37. OLX .... सेवा है?
(a) C2C C (b) C2C
(c) B2C (d) B2B

38. डेबिट कार्ड को एटीएम कार्ड भी कहा जाता है?
(a) True (b) False

39. Who is the investor of Credit Card?
(a) John Biggins, 1946 (b) John Biggins, 1945
(c) John Biggins, 1944 (d) John Biggins, 1943

40. Which key is used for Hyperlink?
(a) Ctrl+K (b) Ctrl+Z
(c) Ctrl+A (d) Ctrl+C

41. Arrange in Ascending order - GB, MB, TB, KB क्या होती है?
(a) KB, MB, GB, TB (b) MB, TB, KB, GB
(c) TB, MB, LB, GB (d) MB, GB, TB, KB

42. Which is the latest Browser?
(a) Google Chrome (b) Firefox
(c) Internet explorer (d) Safari

43. Which one is the First Computer?
(a) ENIAC (b) EDVAC
(c) UNIVAC (d) EDSAC

44. How many people can be added in a one whatsapp group?
(a) 256 (b) 214
(c) 200 (d) 255

45. Which Memory take less access time?
(a) Cache Memory (b) Main Memory
(c) Primary Memory (d) Secondary Memory

46. We can use Operating System in a one computer at a Time?
(a) True (b) False

47. If we want to forward a mail which button we choose?
(a) Forward (b) Send
(c) Close (d) Save

48. Windows is Operating System?
(a) True (b) False

49. Full Form of BHIM?
(a) Bhart Interface For Money
(b) Bharaat Interface For Money
(c) Bhart Intermany For Money
(d) Bhart Interface For Money

50. Bar Code and QR Code एक समान होते हैं?
(a) True (b) False

51. IFSC Code कितने अंक का होता है?

(a) 11 (b) 12
(c) 13 (d) 14

52. APES stand for??
(a) Annual Premium Equivalent
(b) Aadhar Enabled Payment System
(c) Aadhar Payment Enabled System
(d) Aadhar Premium Enabled System

53. ODF का पूर्ण रूप है?
(a) Old Doucment Format
(b) Open Document Format
(c) Open Source Document Format
(d) None of the above

54. CARD का पूर्ण रूप है?
(a) Central for Agricultural and Rural Development
(b) Computer Aided Research and Development
(c) Cumulative Action for Rural Development
(d) All of the above

55. IM का पूर्ण रूप क्या है?
(a) Internet Members (b) Instant Messaging
(c) Including Media (d) None of the above

56. Nasscom का पूर्ण रूप कया है?
(a) National Association of Software and Server Computer
(b) National Association of Software and Serving Computer
(c) National Association of Software and Service Computer
(d) None of these

57. UPI में U क्या है?
(a) University (b) Unified
(c) Unique (d) Universal

58. ATM का पूर्ण रूप क्या है?
(a) Automatic Teller Machine
(b) Automated Teller Machine
(c) Automatic Transmission Money
(d) Automatic Transfer Money

59. CC का पूर्ण रूप क्या है?
(a) Character Code (b) Carbon Code
(c) Carbon Copy (d) None

60. IP का पूर्ण रूप क्या है?
(a) Internet Protocol
(b) Including Protocol
(c) International Protocol
(d) None of the above

61. BFD stand for....?
(a) Binary File Descriptor
(b) Best Finger Detection
(c) Bidirectional Forwarding Detection
(d) All of the above

62. AEPS Full form...?
(a) Aadhaar Electronic Payment System
(b) Aadhaar Enabled Payment System
(c) Advance Enable Payment System
(d) None of the above

63. IMPS का पूर्ण रूप क्या है?
(a) Immediate Payment Service
(b) Immediate Fund Transfer Service
(c) Interested Payment Service
(d) Both (a) and (b)

64. USSD का पूर्ण रूप क्या है?
(a) Unstable Supplementary Service Data
(b) Unstructured Supplementary Service Data
(c) Under Supplementary Service Data
(d) None of the above

65. LibreOffice में कई सॉफ्टवेयर होते हैं?
(a) True (b) False

66. LibreOffice Writer में हाइपरलिंक की शॉर्टकट की क्या है?
(a) Ctrl+K (b) Ctrl+H
(c) Ctrl+L (d) Ctrl+Shift+H

67. पहला सर्च इंजन है?
(a) Yahoo (b) Archie
(c) Altavista (d) Google

68. पहल इलेक्ट्रॉनिक कम्प्यूटर है?
(a) ENIAC (b) Difference Engine
(c) UNIVAC (d) None of the above

69. LibreOffice Impress में न्यूनतम Zoom साइज कितना है?
(a) 5% (b) 10%
(c) 15% (d) 20%

70. फेसबुक क्या है?
(a) ब्राउज़र (b) सर्च इंजिन
(c) मैसेंजर (d) सोशल मीडिया

71. क्या LibreOffice में Ctrl+F का वही काम है जो एमएस ऑफिस में है?
(a) True (b) False

72. Backspace Key से किस तरफ का कैरेक्टर मिटाता है?
(a) Left (b) Right
(c) Both (a) and (b) (d) None of the aboe

73. Shortcut key for new slide...?
(a) Ctrl+M (b) Ctrl+N
(c) Ctrl+D (d) All of the above

74. चीन में कौन सा सर्च इंजन चलता है?
(a) Baidu....Ans (b) Google
(c) Yahoo (d) Bing

75. LibreOffice Writer में redo करने की शॉर्टकट की क्या है?
(a) Ctrl+R (b) Ctrl+Z
(c) Ctrl+Y (d) Ctrl+Shift+R

76. डिलीट किया हुआ ई-मेल कहाँ मिलेगा?
(a) Trash Mail (b) Send Mail
(c) Inbox (d) Outbox

77. इंस्टाग्राम किससे संबंधित है?
(a) Microsoft (b) Google
(c) Facebook (d) Twitter

78. Left Allignment कौन से key द्वारा होता है?
(a) Ctrl+A (b) Ctrl+L
(c) Ctrl+Shift+L (d) None

79. क्लिपबोर्ड क्या है?
(a) एक प्रकार का बोर्ड
(b) हार्डवेयर
(c) कॉपी या कट किए हुए कैरेक्टर सेव होते हैं
(d) None of the above

80. लाइट पैन क्या है?
(a) आउटपुट डिवाइस (b) इनपुट डिवाइस
(c) एक तरह का पैन (d) इनमें से कोई नहीं

81. Bluetooth कोन सा नेटवर्क है?
(a) WAN (b) MAN
(c) PAN (d) LAN

82. QR कोड बार अधिकतम डिजिट होता है?
(a) 7089 (b) 4296
(c) 22953 (d) None

83. IMEI में कितने डिजिट होते हैं?
(a) 10 (b) 12
(c) 13 (d) 15

84. OTP यूज करते हैं?
(a) सुरक्षित लॉगइन (b) सुरक्षित पैसा ट्रांसफर
(c) सुरक्षित ऑनलाइन लेनदेन (d) उपरोक्त सभी

85. LibreOffice शीट को Save as करने की Shortcut Key क्या है?
(a) Ctrl+Shift+S (b) Ctrl+Shift+F
(c) Ctrl+F2 (d) None of the above

86. QR Code यूज होता है?
(a) बैंक खाते की जानकारी
(b) किसी वेबसाइट में log in करने के लिए
(c) पैसा स्थानांतरण करने के लिए
(d) All of above

87. Cell में फॉर्मूल डालने की Shortcut Key है?
(a) Shift+F3 (b) Ctrl+F2
(c) Both (a) and (b) (d) None of the above

88. इनमे से सबसे तेज कौन सी मेमोरी एक्सेस करती है?
(a) Cache Memory (b) Register Memory
(c) Storage Memory (d) Virtual Memory

89. GIGO किससे संबंधित है?
(a) Automatic (b) Accuracy
(c) Flexibility (d) None of the above

90. ASSCII कितने bit का होता है?
(a) 7 bit (b) 8 bit
(c) 16 bit (d) 64 bit

91. क्या कम्प्यूटर में एक से अधिक ऑपरेटिंग सिस्टम हो सकते हैं?
(a) True (b) False

92. एच.टी.टी.पी.एस. में एस. का अर्थ क्या है?
(a) Security (b) Server
(c) Secure (d) Serial

93. हाइपरलिंक करने के लिए शॉर्टकट कुंजी क्या होती है?
(a) Ctrl+K (b) Ctrl+M
(c) Ctrl+Shift+K (d) Ctrl+K+C

94. किसी पंक्ति को कॉलम में किस ऑप्शन के द्वारा बदला जाता है?
(a) Text (b) Change
(c) Transpose (d) Convert

95. MAC Address कितने Bits का होता है?
(a) 6 Bits (b) 24 Bits
(c) 48 Bits (d) 64 Bits

96. इंटरनेट में किस टोपोलॉजी का उपयोग होता है?
(a) Ring (b) Mess
(c) Tree (d) Nota

97. OSI मॉडल में कितनी परते पाई जाती हैं?
(a) 5 (b) 6
(c) 7 (d) 8

98. Excel में एक कॉलम का चयन करने के लिए कौन सी शॉर्टकट कुंजी का इस्तेमाल किया जाएगा?

(a) Shift+Space (b) Ctrl+Space
(c) Alt+Enter (d) Ctrl+Enter

99. टोपोलॉजी का एक प्रकार नहीं है?
(a) रिंग (b) ट्री
(c) मेष नेटवर्क (d) स्टार

100. LibreOffice Calc में Select All करने की शॉर्टकट कुंजी क्या होती है?
(a) Ctrl+Shift+A (b) Ctrl+A
(c) Ctrl+Shift+Space (d) None of the above

Answers

1.	(a)	2.	(c)	3.	(a)	4.	(c)
5.	(a)	6.	(a)	7.	(a)	8.	(b)
9.	(a)	10.	(a)	11.	(d)	12.	(c)
13.	(c)	14.	(b)	15.	(b)	16.	(a)
17.	(c)	18.	(a)	19.	(c)	20.	(c)
21.	(c)	22.	(a)	23.	(a)	24.	(b)
25.	(b)	26.	(b)	27.	(a)	28.	(b)
29.	(b)	30.	(a)	31.	(a)	32.	(a)
33.	(a)	34.	(a)	35.	(a)	36.	(a)
37.	(a)	38.	(a)	39.	(a)	40.	(a)
41.	(a)	42.	(a)	43.	(a)	44.	(a)
45.	(a)	46.	(b)	47.	(a)	48.	(a)
49.	(a)	50.	(b)	51.	(a)	52.	(b)
53.	(b)	54.	(b)	55.	(b)	56.	(c)
57.	(b)	58.	(b)	59.	(c)	60.	(a)
61	(d)	62.	(b)	63.	(a)	64.	(b)
65.	(a)	66.	(a)	67.	(b)	68.	(a)
69.	(a)	70.	(d)	71.	(a)	72.	(a)
73.	(a)	74.	(a)	75.	(c)	76.	(a)
77.	(a)	78.	(b)	79.	(c)	80.	(b)
81.	(C)	82.	(a)	83.	(d)	84.	(d)
85.	(a)	86.	(d)	87.	(c)	88.	(a)
89.	(b)	90.	(a)	91.	(a)	92.	(c)
93.	(a)	94.	(c)	95.	(c)	96.	(b)
97.	(c)	98.	(b)	99.	(b)	100.	(a)

Model Test Paper III

1. **PPT स्लाइड शो के लिए शॉर्टकट कुंजी क्या होती है?**
   (a) F4 (b) F5
   (c) Shift+F5 (d) Ctrl+F5
2. **जस्टिफाई करने की शॉर्टकट कुंजी क्या होती है?**
   (a) Ctrl+Shift+J (b) Ctrl+J
   (c) Ctrl+L (d) Ctrl+R
3. **IMEI नंबर कितने अंक का होता है?**
   (a) 10 (b) 12
   (c) 14 (d) 15
4. **एक साथ कई लोगों को ई-मेल भेज सकते हैं?**
   (a) True (b) False
5. **एम.एल.यू. का पूरा नाम क्या होता है?**
   (a) Arithmetic Logic Unit
   (b) Logical Unit
   (c) Earthmetic Logic Unit
   (d) Arithmetic Unit
6. **उमंग का पूरा नाम क्या है?**
   (a) Unified Mobile Application for New-age Gover-ance
   (b) Unified Mobile Application for New Goverance
   (c) Unified Mobile Application for Network Gover-ance
   (d) Unified Mobile All for New-age Goverance
7. **C2C का पूरा रूप क्या होता है?**
   (a) Customer to Customer
   (b) Client to Client
   (c) Client to Customer
   (d) Customer to Client
8. **लाइनेक्स एक फ्री ओपन सोर्स ऑपरेटिंग सिस्टम है?**
   (a) True (b) False
9. **पेज को नीचे करने के लिए किस कुंजी का इस्तेमाल किया जाता है?**
   (a) Page Up (b) Page Down
   (c) Up (d) Down
10. **क्या हमें अपने पासवर्ड को चेंज करना चाहिए?**
    (a) True (b) False
11. **EDS का पूरा रूप क्या है?**
    (a) Electronic Data Software
    (b) Electronic Data System
    (c) Electric Data System
    (d) Electric Digit System
12. **इंस्टाग्राम पर कितनी देर का वीडियो रिकॉर्ड करके पोस्ट किया जा सकता है?**
    (a) 30 second (b) 60 second
    (c) 5 minute (d) 2 minute
13. **MAC का पूरा नाम क्या है?**
    (a) Media Access Control Address
    (b) Mac Access Control Address
    (c) Machenical Access Control Address
    (d) More Access Control Address
14. **यू.पी.आई. पिन कितने अंक का होता है?**
    (a) 3 (b) 4
    (c) 5 (d) 6
15. **Full Form of VGA?**
    (a) Video Graphic Area
    (b) Viral Graphic Area
    (c) Video Group Area
    (d) Video Graphic All
16. **Full Form of VPN?**
    (a) Virtual Private Network
    (b) Visual Private Network
    (c) View Private Network
    (d) Virtual Personal Network
17. **Short cut key of Print Preview?**
    (a) Ctrl+Shift+O (b) Ctrl+O
    (c) Ctrl+2 (d) Ctrl+A
18. **Full Form of MICR?**
    (a) Magnetic Ink Character Recognition
    (b) Magnet Ink Character Recognition
    (c) Magnetic Ink Code Reader
    (d) Magnetic Ink Character Row
19. **UPI से Received Money क्या कहलाता है?**
    (a) Full (b) Null
    (c) Received (d) Credited
20. **Full Form of PoS?**
    (a) Point of Sale (b) Point of Switch
    (c) Point of Salary (d) Power of Sale
21. **Libre Office का Word Processing Software का नाम है?**
    (a) Writer (b) Impress
    (c) Word (d) Calc

22. Whatsapp is IM?
(a) True (b) False

23. Facebook is Social Networking?
(a) True (b) False

24. Original Name of Twitter?
(a) twttr (b) twit
(c) twitt (d) twitr

25. Full Form of DNS?
(a) Domain Name System
(b) Define Name System
(c) Domain None System
(d) Domain Name Sale

26. AEPS में P का मतलब है?
(a) Payment (b) Pay
(c) Pay e (d) Pay of k

27. What is IBM 1401?
(a) Mainframe Computer
(b) Micro Computer
(c) Mini Computer
(d) Mac Computer

28. Full Form of USSD?
(a) Unstructured Supplementary Service
(b) Unstructured Service Supplementary
(c) Undefine Supplementary Service
(d) Unnecessary Supplementary Service

29. Libre Office मे Window Close करने की Key?
(a) Ctrl+W (b) Ctrl+X
(c) Ctrl+A (d) Ctrl+Z

30. क्या Libre Office में Ctrl+F का वही काम है जो MS Office में होता है?
(a) True (b) False

31. क्या Safari एक Web Browser है?
(a) True (b) False

32. China में कौन सा सर्च इंजन इस्तेमाल होता है?
(a) Biadu (b) Internet Explorer
(c) Safari (d) Chrome

33. 8 Bit =?
(a) 1 Byte (b) 2 Byte
(c) 3 Byte (d) 40 Byte

34. Delete Email को कहाँ से प्राप्त कर सकते हैं?
(a) Trash Folder (b) Recycle Bin
(c) Downloads (d) Desk to P

35. Short cut key of Redo in Libre Office?
(a) Ctrl+Y (b) Ctrl+L
(c) Ctrl+A (d) Ctrl+X

36. पेज ब्रेक करने की शॉर्टकट की है?
(a) Shift+Enter (b) Ctrl+Enter
(c) Enter (d) None of these

37. Libre Office Writer में प्रिंट प्रीव्यू की शॉर्टकट की क्या है?
(a) Ctrl+Shift+O (b) Ctrl+F2
(c) Ctrl+Shift+P (d) Ctrl+P

38. UTR का पूर्ण रूप क्या है?
(a) Unique Transfer Reference
(b) Uniquely Transaction Reference
(c) Unique Transaction Reference
(d) None of the above

39. ULSI, LSI, VLSI का प्रयोग किस पीढ़ी में किया गया?
(a) First (b) Second
(c) Third (d) Fourth

40. कौन सा नेटवर्क countries, cities, world को कनेक्ट करता है?
(a) LAN (b) WAN
(c) PAN (d) MAN

41. Solve Max where A1 to A3 range?
(a) Max(A1:A3) (b) Max(A1-A3)
(c) Max(A1,A3) (d) Max(A1*A3)

42. Find = quotient(5,2)?
(a) 2 (b) 3
(c) 6 (d) 8

43. Facebook Account ओपन करने की न्यूनतम उम्र होनी चाहिए?
(a) 13 (b) 14
(c) 12 (d) 18

44. OLX क्या है?
(a) e commerce (b) e goverence
(c) e-mail (d) none of the above

45. कम्प्यूटर में PAN का पूर्णरूप क्या है?
(a) Personal Area Network
(b) Permanent Account Number
(c) Permanent Area Network
(d) None of the above

46. Column को सिलेक्ट करने की शॉर्टकट की क्या है?
(a) Ctrl+Spacebar (b) Shift+Spacebar
(c) Shift++ (d) Ctrl++

47. Left Click करके सभी स्लाइड पर ले जाने से क्या होता है?
(a) Selecting (b) Moving
(c) Dragging (d) None of the above

48. भीम एप द्वारा अधिकतम एक दिन में कितना अमाउंट ट्रांसफर कर सकते हैं?
(a) 10000 (b) 20000
(c) 40000 (d) 100000

49. Phone Pay क्या है?
(a) NIC Card (b) E Wallet
(c) Messenger (d) All of the above

50. Thesaurus के लिए शॉर्टकट की क्या है?
(a) Shift+F7 (b) F7
(c) F5 (d) Shift+F5

51. RDS का पूर्ण रूप क्या है?
(a) Reboot Desktop Services
(b) Remote Desktop Services
(c) Remote Desktop Server
(d) None of the above

52. MS World & Writer में सबसे नीचे जो दिखाई देता है उसे क्या बोलते हैं?
(a) Status Bar (b) Title Bar
(c) Task Bar (d) Menu Bar

53. UPI Pin कितने डिजिट का होता है?
(a) 4 (b) 4-6
(c) 6 (d) 8

54. LAN MAN WAN का प्रयोग किस पीढ़ी में किया गया?
(a) First (b) Second
(c) Third (d) Fourth

55. IC का निर्माण किसने किया?
(a) बिल गेट्स (b) जैक किल्बी
(c) मार्क एंडरसन (d) हरमन हेलोरीत

56. AI किस जेनरेशन से संबंधित है?
(a) First Generation (b) Third Generation
(c) Fifth Generation (d) Sixth Generation

57. Libre Office में Word Count कहाँ पर दिखाई देता है?
(a) Task Bar (b) Title Bar
(c) Status Bar (d) None

58. When NEFT is established?
(a) November 2005 (b) November 2006
(c) November 2007 (d) November 2008

59. इनमें से क्या Cyber Attack है?
(a) MiTm (b) Phishing
(c) Reply Attack (d) Wire Sniffing

60. .gov, .edu, .nic, are called?
(a) डोमेन नेम एक्टेंशन (b) फाइल एक्सटेंशन
(c) डोमेन नेम (d) आईपी ऐड्रेस

61. EEROM का पूर्ण रूप है?
(a) Electric Erasable Read-Only Memory
(b) Electronic Erasable Read-Only Memory
(c) Electrically Erasable Read-Only Memory
(d) None of the above

62. We can use gmail... जीमेल को यूज कर सकते हैं...?
(a) Only on Monday (b) 24*7
(c) Yearly (d) Weekly

63. Libre Office Calc अधिकतम Zoom नहीं कर सकते हैं?
(a) 200 (b) 300
(c) 400 (d) 500

64. Libre Office में Calc को कहा जाता है?
(a) Spreadsheet (b) Impress
(c) Calculator (d) Word

65. E-mail को प्रोटेक्ट करने के लिए हमें किसका उसे करते हैं?
(a) PGP Password
(b) GP Password
(c) PP Password
(d) PG Password

66. IE stand for??
(a) Internet Explorer (b) Interest Explorer
(c) Involve Explorer (d) Invest Extra

67. How many worksheet on Libreoffice calc by default?
(a) One (b) Two
(c) Three (d) Four

68. Minimum font size in libre office writer?
(a) 999.9 (b) 100
(c) 909 (d) 10000

69. First Web Browser?
(a) WWW (b) WW
(c) HTML (d) Google

70. How many parts of e-mail ID?
(a) Two (b) Three
(c) Four (d) Five

71. What is fireball?
(a) Hardware or Software
(b) Jammer
(c) Hardware
(d) Software

72. Keylogger is a......?

(a) Spyware (b) Virus
(c) Malware (d) Hacker

73. Full form of IFSC code?

(a) Indian Financial System Code, 11 digits
(b) Indian Financial System Code, 12 digits
(c) Indian Financial System Code, 14 digits
(d) Indian Financial System Code, 16 digits

74. For which card we pay advance payment?

(a) Prepaid Card (b) Postpaid Card
(c) Pre Card (d) Post Card

75. IMEI no. is used for?

(a) Identify valid device
(b) Identify value device
(c) Identify val device
(d) Indian valid device

76. Full form of EBCDIC?

(a) Extended Binary Coded Decimal Interchange Code
(b) Extended Big Coded Decimal Interchange Code
(c) Extended Binary Code Decimal Interchange Code
(d) Extended Binary Coded Digit Interchange Code

77. Twitter is which type of site?

(a) Micro Blogging (b) Mini Blogging
(c) Blog (d) Vebpage

78. =Ceilling(120,11)?

(a) 14 (b) 15
(c) 16 (d) 17

79. What is the shortcut key of auto correct?

(a) Alt+F7 (b) Ctrl+A
(c) Ctrl+2 (d) Ctrl+O

80. Normal view is in which menu?

(a) View Menu (b) File Menu
(c) Save Menu (d) Edit Menu

81. Shortcut key to reach to last edit cell in Libreoffice Calc?

(a) Ctrl+End (b) Ctrl+A
(c) Ctrl+Z (d) Ctrl+O

82. Domain name for education institutions?

(a) ac (b) cc
(c) db (d) vc

83. Strikethrough is from which menu?

(a) Format (b) File
(c) View (d) Edit

84. Which memory in CPU?

(a) Registers (b) Primary
(c) Secondary (d) Cache

85. Which is app we use for search place & directions?

(a) Google Map (b) Google View
(c) Google Street View (d) Google Chrome

86. Key for reach beginning of the line in Libreoffice writer?

(a) Home (b) End
(c) Enter (d) Space Bar

87. Shortcut key for permanent delete any file without send it recyclebin?

(a) Shift+Del (b) Shift+Act
(c) Shift+Z (d) Shift+A

88. E-wallet use for?

(a) Digital Payment (b) Dot Payment
(c) Digit Payment (d) Digital Payee

89. MMID code has how many numbers?

(a) Mobile Money Identifier, 7 digit
(b) Mobile Money Identifier, 8 digit
(c) Mobile Money Identifier, 9 digit
(d) Mobile Money Identifier, 10 digit

90. IMPAS full form?

(a) Immediate Payment Service
(b) Immediate Payee Service
(c) Inter Payment Service
(d) In Payment Service

91. Full form of IP?

(a) Internet Protocol (b) Inter Protocol
(c) Internet Practice (d) Internet Project

92. Instagram किससे संबंधित है?

(a) Facebook (b) Watsap
(c) Twitter (d) Instant Messaging

93. When we hide and slide on Power Point?

(a) True (b) False

94. Folders are Directories?

(a) True (b) False

95. क्या आप Message में बिना विषय के संदेश लिखकर msg भेज सकते हैं?

(a) True (b) False

96. लिब्रे ऑफिस एक एप्लीकेशन सॉफ्टवेयर है?

(a) True (b) False

97. QR code phone pe में उपलब्ध होता है?

(a) True (b) False

98. पर्सनल कम्प्यूटर कौन सा है?

(a) मिनी कम्प्यूटर (b) माइक्रो कम्प्यूटर

(c) सुपर कम्प्यूटर (d) कोई भी नहीं

99. Libreoffice में कट करने की शॉर्टकट की क्या है?

(a) Ctrl+C (b) Ctrl+S

(c) Ctrl+X (d) Shift+X

100. वेक्यूम ट्यूब का आविष्कार कब हुआ?

(a) 1904 (b) 1954

(c) 1946 (d) 1960

Answers

1.	(a)	2.	(b)	3.	(d)	4.	(a)
5.	(a)	6.	(a)	7.	(a)	8.	(a)
9.	(b)	10.	(a)	11.	(b)	12.	(b)
13.	(a)	14.	(d)	15.	(a)	16.	(a)
17.	(a)	18.	(a)	19.	(d)	20.	(a)
21.	(a)	22.	(a)	23.	(a)	24.	(a)
25.	(a)	26.	(a)	27.	(a)	28.	(a)
29.	(b)	30.	(a)	31.	(a)	32.	(a)
33.	(a)	34.	(a)	35.	(a)	36.	(b)
37.	(a)	38.	(c)	39.	(d)	40.	(b)
41.	(a)	42.	(a)	43.	(a)	44.	(a)
45.	(a)	46.	(b)	47.	(b)	48.	(c)
49.	(b)	50.	(a)	51.	(b)	52.	(a)
53.	(b)	54.	(d)	55.	(b)	56.	(c)
57.	(c)	58.	(a)	59.	(a)	60.	(a)
61	(c)	62.	(b)	63.	(d)	64.	(a)
65.	(a)	66.	(a)	67.	(a)	68.	(a)
69.	(a)	70.	(a)	71.	(a)	72.	(a)
73.	(a)	74.	(a)	75.	(a)	76.	(a)
77.	(a)	78.	(a)	79.	(a)	80.	(a)
81.	(a)	82.	(a)	83.	(a)	84.	(a)
85.	(a)	86.	(a)	87.	(a)	88.	(a)
89.	(a)	90.	(a)	91.	(a)	92.	(a)
93.	(b)	94.	(a)	95.	(a)	96.	(a)
97.	(a)	98.	(b)	99.	(c)	100.	(a)

Model Test Paper IV

1. **पहला माइक्रो एटीएम आधार बेस्ड किस बैंक ने शुरू किया?**
   (a) State Bank of Patiala
   (b) Kotak Mahindra Bank
   (c) Axis Bank
   (d) ICICI Bank

2. **Umang एप्लीकेशन किस मंत्रालय ने शुरू किया था?**
   (a) Ministry of Electronics & IT
   (b) Ministry of HRD
   (c) Ministry of Finance
   (d) All of the above

3. **पहला ग्राफिक्स वेब ब्राउज़र कौन है?**
   (a) World Wide Web (b) Mosaic
   (c) Netscape (d) Safari

4. **SED stand for?**
   (a) Smoke Editor
   (b) Smoke-Emitting Diode
   (c) Sweet Eagle Diode
   (d) All of the above

5. **कौन सी कुंजी का संयोजन दूसरी कुंजी से किया जाए जिससे दस्तावेज में अंतर दिखाई दे?**
   (a) Function (b) Sift
   (c) Caps Lock (d) Ctrl

6. **Pocket wallet किस बैंक ने स्टार्ट किया?**
   (a) HDFC Bank
   (b) ICICI Bank
   (c) State Bank of India
   (d) Punjab National Bank

7. **=sum(5,2) कितना होता है?**
   (a) 1 (b) 3
   (c) 7 (d) 10

8. **Whatsapp ग्रुप में अधिकतम कितने सदस्य होते हैं?**
   (a) 250 (b) 255
   (c) 256 (d) No Limit

9. **Libreoffice Writer डिफॉल्ट फाइल एक्सटेंशन क्या है?**
   (a) .ods (b) .odt
   (c) .odp (d) .docx

10. **USSD का पूर्ण रूप क्या है?**
    (a) Unstructured Supplementary Service Data
    (b) Uniform Supplementary Service Data
    (c) United Supplementary Service Data
    (d) Universal Supplementary Service Data

11. **P2P क्या है?**
    (a) Point to Point (b) Peer to Peer
    (c) Point to Pest (d) None of the above

12. **PIN का पूर्णरूप क्या है?**
    (a) Permanent Internet Number
    (b) Personal Identification Number
    (c) Permanent Identifiation Number
    (d) None of the above

13. **RTGS का पूर्णरूप क्या है?**
    (a) Right Time Gross Settlement
    (b) Real Time Gross Sales
    (c) Real Time Gross Settlement
    (d) None of the above

14. **HTTP में TT क्या है?**
    (a) Test Transfer (b) Text Transfer
    (c) Test Transformed (d) None of the above

15. **Libreoffice विंडो को बंद करने के लिए शॉर्टकट की क्या होती है?**
    (a) Ctrl+Q (b) Ctrl+W
    (c) Ctrl+Shift+W (d) None of the above

16. **Twitter के Logo में क्या होता है?**
    (a) जानवर (b) चिड़िया
    (c) T लिखा हुआ (d) इनमें से कोई नहीं

17. **मोबाइल फोन किसके द्वारा Track किया जा सकता है?**
    (a) IMEI (b) GPS
    (c) Both (d) None of the above

18. **NABARD किस कमेटी द्वारा Established किया गया?**
    (a) Harsh Kumar Committee
    (b) B. Sivaraman Committee
    (c) 1982 Act Committee
    (d) Rama Rao Committee

19. **LibreOffice Impress में स्लाइड सॉर्टर किस मेनू में पाया जाता है?**
    (a) Insert (b) View
    (c) Home (d) Format

20. **POS का पूर्ण रूप क्या है?**
    (a) Post of Sales (b) Point of Sales
    (c) Point of Sold (d) None of the abobe

21. **Cryptography क्या है?**
    (a) यह हमारे डाटा को सुरक्षित रखता है
    (b) डाटा को सीक्रेट कोड में बदल देता है
    (c) इसका इस्तेमाल ईमेल डेबिट कार्ड क्रेडिट कार्ड में होता है
    (d) उपरोक्त सभी

22. **अगली स्लाइड पर जाने की शॉर्टकट की क्या है?**
    (a) Home (b) End
    (c) PageUp (d) PageDown

23. **फेसबुक के फाउंडर कौन हैं?**
    (a) जैक डोर्सी (b) मार्क जुकरबर्ग
    (c) बिल गेट्स (d) लैरी पेज

24. **CD-RW क्या है?**
    (a) सिर्फ पढ़ सकते हैं
    (b) लिख सकते हैं
    (c) लिख और पढ़ सकते हैं
    (d) पढ़ सकते है लिख सकते हैं दोबारा लिख सकते हैं

25. **Yahoo Messenger, Instant Messaging का उदाहरण है?**
    (a) True (b) False

26. **Safari एक सर्च इंजन है?**
    (a) True (b) False

27. **UPI नकदी लेनदेन को बढ़ावा देता है?**
    (a) True (b) False

28. **क्या पालतू जानवरों के नाम का पासवर्ड बनाना चाहिए?**
    (a) True (b) False

29. **UMANG App में N से क्या तात्पर्य है?**
    (a) New Age (b) New Group
    (c) New (d) No Age

30. **Libre Office Writer में किसी भी लाइन की शुरूआत में जाने की शॉर्टकट Key क्या है?**
    (a) Home (b) Ctrl + Home
    (c) Up (d) PageUp

31. **Libreoffice Calc में =CEILING(120,11) का मान कितना होगा?**
    (a) 120 (b) 121
    (c) 122 (d) 130

32. **Calc में अधिकतम zoom कितना होता है?**
    (a) 300% (b) 3000%
    (c) 500% (d) 400%

33. **लिब्रा ऑफिस Calc स्प्रेडशीट फाइल एक्सटेंशन क्या है?**
    (a) .ods (b) .odp
    (c) odt (d) odd

34. **Libreoffice calc में save as की शॉर्टकट की क्या है?**
    (a) Ctrl+Shift+S (b) Ctrl+S
    (c) Ctrl+Shift+O (d) Ctrl+Alt+S

35. **Libreoffice writer में CUT की शॉर्टकट की क्या है?**
    (a) Ctrl+Shift+C (b) Ctrl+C
    (c) Ctrl+X (d) None of these

36. **Libreoffice calc में Select all की शॉर्ट की क्या है?**
    (a) Ctril+Shift+A (b) Ctrl+A
    (c) Ctrl+Shift+Space (d) None of these

37. **Libreoffice writer में Select all की शॉर्ट की क्या है?**
    (a) Ctril+Shift+A (b) Ctrl+A
    (c) Ctrl+Shift+Space (d) None of these

38. **Impress में टेक्स्ट बॉक्स के लिए किस key का प्रयोग करते हैं?**
    (a) Ctrl+F2 (b) F3
    (c) Shift+F2 (d) F2

39. **Jump to Last edited slide पर जाने की शॉर्टकट की क्या है?**
    (a) Ctrl+Number (b) Alt+Shift+F5
    (c) Shift+F5 (d) None of these

40. **Calc में कितने रो और कॉलम होते है?**
    (a) 1024 & 1048576 (b) 1048576 & 1024
    (c) 1048576 & 16384 (d) 16384 & 1048576

41. **लिब्रा ऑफिस Current Window Close की शॉर्टकट की क्या है?**
    (a) Ctrl+W (b) Ctrl+Q
    (c) Ctrl+T (d) None of these

42. **लिब्रा ऑफिस से बाहर निकलने की शॉर्टकट की क्या है?**
    (a) Ctrl+W (b) Ctrl_Q
    (c) Ctrl+T (d) None of these

43. **Libreoffice draw में duplicate shape की शॉर्टकट की क्या होती है?**
    (a) Shift+F3 (b) Ctrl+Shift+Q
    (c) Ctrl+Alt+O (d) None of these

44. **Libreoffice draw में ruler की शॉर्टकट की क्या है?**
    (a) Shift+F3 (b) Ctrl+Shift+R
    (c) Ctrl+Alt+O (d) None of these

45. **Libreoffice draw में hyperlink की शॉर्टकट की क्या है?**
    (a) Ctrl+K (b) Ctrl+Shift+R
    (c) Ctrl+Alt+K (d) None of these

46. **Libreoffice calc में full screen mode की शॉर्टकट की क्या है?**

(a) Ctrl+Shift+F11 (b) Ctrl+Shift+J
(c) F11 (d) Nota

47. Libreoffice calc में insert function की शॉर्टकट की क्या है?
(a) Shift+F3 (b) Ctrl+F2
(c) Ctrl+F3 (d) None of these

48. Libreoffice calc में comment insert की शॉर्टकट की क्या है?
(a) Shift+F3 (b) Ctrl+F2
(c) Ctrl+Alt+C (d) None of these

49. लिब्रा ऑफिस में Automatic Spell Checking के लिए किस शॉर्टकट key का प्रयोग करते है?
(a) Shift+F7 (b) F7
(c) F6 (d) Ctrl+F7

50. Writer में सिलेक्टेड टेक्स्ट पर heading 1 स्टाइल लगाने के लिए किस शॉर्टकट की का प्रयोग किया जाता है?
(a) Ctrl+1 (b) Ctrl+H
(c) Ctrl+Shift+T (d) Nota

51. Writer में अधिकतम Zoom कितना होता है?
(a) 300% (b) 400%
(c) 400% (d) 3000%

52. Impress में अधिकतम Zoom कितना होता है?
(a) 300% (b) 400%
(c) 500% (d) 3000%

53. एक समय में एक कथन को कन्वर्ट और एग्जीक्यूट करता है?
(a) कनवर्टर (b) कंपाइलर
(c) इंटरप्रेटर (d) असेंबलर

54. कट कॉपी और पेस्ट आदि कार्य किस मेनू के द्वारा किए जाते हैं?
(a) इंसर्ट मेनू (b) एडिट
(c) फॉरमैट (d) फाइल

55. UPI द्वारा अधिकतम कितना पैसा ट्रांसफर कर सकते हैं?
(a) 10,000 (b) 20,000
(c) 50,000 (d) 1,00,000

56. PMSBY का पूर्ण रूप क्या है?
(a) Pradhan Mantri Security Bima Yojna
(b) Pradhan Mantri Secure Bima Yojna
(c) Pradhan Mantri Suraksha Bima Yojna
(d) None of these

57. NEFT/RTGS द्वारा कितना पैसा ट्रांसफर कर सकते हैं?
(a) More than 200000 (b) 500000
(c) 1000000 (d) No Limit

58. क्रेडिट कार्ड हमें क्या प्रदान करता है?
(a) Cash (b) Cheque
(c) Cheque or Cash Both (d) None the above

59. इंटरनेट के फाउंडर कौन है?
(a) ARPA (b) IMB
(c) Tim Berners Lee (d) Charles Babbage

60. वर्ल्ड का पहला सुपर कम्प्यूटर का क्या नाम है?
(a) CDC 6600 (b) Cray 1
(c) UNIVAC (d) Summit

61. आउटबॉक्स और सेंटबॉक्स एक समान होते हैं?
(a) True (b) False

62. इंटरनेट क्या है?
(a) नेटवर्क सिस्टम (b) वेबसाइट का ग्रुप
(c) वेब पेज का ग्रुप (d) सॉफ्टवेयर

63. इंटरनेट का मालिक है?
(a) True (b) False

64. Calc में Cell की अधिकतम ऊँचाई होती है?
(a) 0.45 inch (b) 0.45 cm
(c) 1.25 inch (d) 1.25 cm

65. निम्नलिखित में से अलग कौन सी है?
(a) सेंट्रल बैंक (b) यूनियन बैंक
(c) स्टेट बैंक ऑफ इंडिया (d) रिजर्व बैंक ऑफ इंडिया

66. निम्नलिखित में 3D में D का मतलब क्या है?
(a) Division (b) Display
(c) Dimension (d) Discover

67. Proprietary सॉफ्टवेयर का दूसरा नाम क्या है?
(a) Open Source Software
(b) Closed Source Software
(c) Paid Software
(d) Freeware

68. DARPA क्या है?
(a) अमेरिका की डिफेंस संगठन
(b) इंटरनेट का निर्माण किया
(c) Defense Advanced Research Project Agency
(d) All of the above

69. CD का आविष्कार किसने किया?
(a) Jems T. Russel (b) Marc Anthony
(c) Tim Berners Lee (d) None of the above

70. TFT का पूर्ण रूप क्या है?
(a) Thick Film Transistor
(b) Thin Film Transistor
(c) Tubular Film Transistor

(d) None of the above

71 आधार कार्ड में कितने डिजिट होते हैं?

(a) 10 (b) 12
(c) 14 (d) 15

72 कौन सा नेटवर्क बिल्डिंग के कैंपस तक सीमित है?

(a) LAN (b) WAN
(c) MAN (d) All of the above

73 NUUP पूर्ण रूप क्या है?

(a) National Unified USSD Platform
(b) National Unifier USSD Platorm
(c) National Universal USSD Platform
(d) None of the above

74 स्प्रेडशीट के पहले Cell में पहुँचने के लिए शॉर्टकट Key क्या है?

(a) Ctrl+Home (b) Shift+Home
(c) Home (d) Ctrl+PageUp

75 ट्विटर हैंड Symbol क्या है?

(a) $ (b) #
(c) @ (d) Nota

76 जीमेल से हम अधिकतम कितने MB तक अटैचमेंट भेज सकते हैं?

(a) 15 (b) 20
(c) 25 (d) 30

77 किस कार्ड के लिए पहले से भुगतान करना पड़ता है?

(a) Credit Card (b) Debit Card
(c) Gold Card (d) All above

78 अगर मारूति MRF से टायर खरीदती है तो किस प्रकार का व्यवसाय है?

(a) Customer to Customer
(b) Business to Business
(c) Business to Customer
(d) Customer to Business

79 दो दोस्तों की ईमेल आईडी समान हो सकती है?

(a) True (b) False

80 Email के फाउंडर कौन हैं?

(a) Bill Gates (b) Ray Tomlinson
(c) Steve Jobs (d) None of the above

81 Duckduckgo क्या है?

(a) Web Browser (b) Search Engine
(c) Bird Name (d) Network

82 WhatsApp हम कभी भी कितनी बार नंबर बदल सकते हैं?

(a) True (b) False

83 Swift क्या है?

(a) Society for Worldwide Interbank Financial Telecommunication code
(b) इसका प्रयोग विदेशों में पैसा ट्रांसफर करने के लिए किया जाता है
(c) दोनों
(d) कोई नहीं

84 UPI NCPI द्वारा स्थापित है?

(a) True (b) False

85 B कॉलम को जोड़ने का कौन सा फॉर्मूला सही है?

(a) =add(B1:B1048576)
(b) =sum(B1:B1048576)
(c) =sum(B1,B10484576)
(d) None of the above

86 Libre Office Row की कुल संख्या है?

(a) 1024 (b) 10678
(c) 1084576 (d) 1048576

87 Blockchain टेक्नोलॉजी क्या है?

(a) सुरक्षित लेनदेन में सहायक
(b) बिटकॉयन में इस्तेमाल होने वाली टेक्नोलॉजी है
(c) Both of the above
(d) None of the above

88 डिस्क्रिप्शन और एंक्रिप्शन का प्रदर्शन क्या है?

(a) यह हमारे डाटा को सुरक्षित रखता है
(b) सुरक्षित लेनदेन में सहायक
(c) दोनों
(d) कोई नहीं

89 इनमें से कौन सबसे अच्छा विश्वकोष (Encylopedia) है?

(a) Wikipedia (b) Google
(c) Quora (d) Yahoo

90 DES का पूर्ण रूप क्या है?

(a) Data Encryption Slot
(b) Data Encryption Solution
(c) Data Encryption Standard
(d) None of the above

91 हेडिंग 3 के लिए शॉर्टकट की है?

(a) Ctrl+3 (b) Shift+3
(c) Shift+1 (d) Ctrl+1

92 निम्नलिखित में से कौन सा वेब ब्राउज़र है?

(a) गूगल (b) याहू
(c) यूट्यूब (d) मोज़िला फायरफॉक्स

93 **DOS GUI पर आधारित है?**

(a) True (b) False

94 **File नेम और Extension के बीच में क्या लगाकर अलग करते हैं?**

(a) @ (b) .(dot)
(c) # (d) $

95 **क्रेडिट करना किससे संबंधित है?**

(a) बैंक में पैसे जमा करना (b) Cash निकालना
(c) Debit (d) None of these

96 **फेसबुक में अधिकतम कितने फ्रेंड हो सकते हैं?**

(a) 256 (b) 1000
(c) 5000 (d) No limiyt

97 **बैंक को इंटरनेट से कब अटैच किया गया?**

(a) 1994 (b) 1995
(c) 1996 (d) 2000

98 **सफारी एक सर्च इंजन है?**

(a) True (b) False

99 **CPU में कौन सी स्टोरेज डिवाइस लगी होती है?**

(a) ट्रांजिस्टर (b) कैश मेमोरी
(c) हार्ड डिस्क (d) सभी

100 **NEFT की टाइमिंग क्या है?**

(a) 6:30 am to 6.00 pm
(b) 8:00 am to 6:00 pm
(c) 8:00 am to 7:00 pm
(d) None of the above

Answers

1.	(c)	2.	(a)	3.	(b)	4.	(c)
5.	(d)	6.	(b)	7.	(c)	8.	(c)
9.	(b)	10.	(a)	11.	(b)	12.	(b)
13.	(c)	14.	(b)	15.	(a)	16.	(b)
17.	(c)	18.	(b)	19.	(b)	20.	(b)
21.	(d)	22.	(d)	23.	(b)	24.	(d)
25.	(a)	26.	(b)	27.	(a)	28.	(b)
29.	(a)	30.	(a)	31.	(b)	32.	(c)
33.	(b)	34.	(a)	35.	(a)	36.	(a)
37.	(b)	38.	(d)	39.	(b)	40.	(b)
41.	(a)	42.	(b)	43.	(a)	44.	(b)
45.	(a)	46.	(b)	47.	(a)	48.	(c)
49.	(a)	50.	(a)	51.	(b)	52.	(d)
53.	(c)	54.	(b)	55.	(d)	56.	(c)
57.	(d)	58.	(c)	59.	(a)	60.	(a)
61	(b)	62.	(a)	63.	(b)	64.	(c)
65.	(d)	66.	(c)	67.	(b)	68.	(d)
69.	(a)	70.	(b)	71.	(b)	72.	(a)
73.	(a)	74.	(a)	75.	(c)	76.	(c)
77.	(b)	78.	(b)	79.	(b)	80.	(b)
81.	(b)	82.	(a)	83.	(c)	84.	(a)
85.	(b)	86.	(d)	87.	(c)	88.	(c)
89.	(a)	90.	(c)	91.	(a)	92.	(d)
93.	(b)	94.	(b)	95.	(a)	96.	(c)
97.	(c)	98.	(b)	99.	(d)	100.	(c)

Model Test Paper V

1. ट्विटर में # का क्या यूज होता है?
   (a) किसी को टैग करना
   (b) किसी विषय पर चर्चा करना
   (c) किसी को मैसेज करना
   (d) उपरोक्त सभी

2. क्रेडिट कार्ड में APR क्या है?
   (a) Interest Rate
   (b) Annual Percentage Rage
   (c) Both (a) and (b)
   (d) None of the above

3. UMANG का पूर्ण रूप क्या है?
   (a) Unified Mobile Application for New-age Goverance
   (b) Universal Mobile Application for New-age Goverance
   (c) Unifier Mobile Application for New-age Goverance
   (d) None of the above

4. क्या जानवरों के नाम का पासवर्ड रखना चाहिए?
   (a) True (b) False

5. लिब्रे ऑफिस एप्लीकेशन सॉफ्टवेयर नहीं है?
   (a) True (b) False

6. BHIM App के द्वारा एक दिन में कितने पैसे भेजें जा सकते हैं?
   (a) 10000 (b) 20000
   (c) 40000 (d) No limit

7. Calc का फाइल एक्सटेंशन?
   (a) .odc (b) .odt
   (c) .ods (d) .odp

8. TCP/IP में कितने लेयर होते हैं?
   (a) 3 (b) 4
   (c) 5 (d) 7

9. क्या हम एक पीसी पर दो ऑपरेटिंग सिस्टम यूज कर सकते हैं?
   (a) True (b) False

10. FTP में F का मतलब क्या होता है?
    (a) File (b) Font
    (c) Format (d) Function

11. IPV6 Address Bits... .
    (a) 28 (b) 32
    (c) 64 (d) 128

12. इंस्टाग्राम के फाउंडर कौन हैं?
    (a) Bill Gates
    (b) Marc Zuckerberg
    (c) Kavin Systrom and Mike Krieger
    (d) None of the above

13. Mac Addresses size
    (a) 6 byte (b) 12 digits
    (c) 48 bits (d) All

14. फंक्शन के अंदर फंक्शन को क्या कहते हैं?
    (a) Function (b) Nested Function
    (c) General Function (d) Condition Function

15. एनालॉग और डिजिटल कम्प्यूटर का मिक्स रूप है?
    (a) Super Computer (b) Personal Computer
    (c) Hybrid Computer (d) None of the above

16. पहले स्लाइड पर जाने की शॉर्टकट की क्या है?
    (a) Pageup (b) Pagedown
    (c) Home (d) End

17. Full Form of set...
    (a) Security end Technology
    (b) Secure Electronic Transactions
    (c) Security Electronics Transactions
    (d) None of the above

18. Cloud Computinh क्या है?
    (a) अपने डाटा को इंटरनेट पर सुरक्षित करना
    (b) डाटा को कम्प्यूटर में सेव करना
    (c) कम्प्यूटर के इंटरनेट से जोड़ना
    (d) All of the above

19. LibreOffice में कई सॉफ्टवेयर होते हैं?
    (a) True (b) False

20. LibreOffice Writer में हाइपर लिंक की शॉर्टकट की क्या है?
    (a) Ctrl+K (b) Ctrl+H
    (c) Ctrl+L (d) Ctrl+Shift+H

21. IMPS का पूर्ण रूप क्या है?
    (a) Immediate fund transfer service
    (b) Immediate payment service
    (c) Interested payment service
    (d) Both (a) and (b)

22. पहला सर्च इंजन है?

(a) Yahoo (b) Archie
(c) Altavista (d) Google

23. पहला इलेक्ट्रॉनिक कम्प्यूटर है:
(a) ENIAC (b) UNIVAC
(c) Difference Engine (d) None of the above

24. LibreOffice Impress में न्यूनतम zoom साइज कितना है?
(a) 5% (b) 10%
(c) 15% (d) 20%

25. फेसबुक क्या है?
(a) सर्च इंजन (b) ब्राउजर
(c) मैसेंजर (d) सोशल मीडिया

26. क्या LibreOffice में Ctrl+F का वही काम है जो एमएस ऑफिस में है?
(a) True (b) False

27. Full form of AEPS...
(a) Advanced Enable Payment System
(b) Aadhaar Enabled Payment System
(c) Aadhaar Electronic Payment System
(d) None of the above

28. USSD का पूर्णरूप क्या है?
(a) Unstructured Supplementary Service Data
(b) Unstable Supplementary Service Data
(c) Under Supplementary Service Data
(d) None of the above

29. Backspace कुंजी से किस तरफ का कैरेक्टर मिटाता है?
(a) बाएं (b) दाएं
(c) दोनों (d) कोई नहीं

30. BFD stand for:
(a) Binary File Descriptor
(b) Best Finger Detection
(c) Bidirectional Forwarding Detection
(d) All of above

31. Shortcut key for new slide:
(a) Ctrl+M (b) Ctrl+N
(c) Ctrl+D (d) All

32. चीन में कौन सा सर्च इंजन चलता है?
(a) Baidu (b) Google
(c) Yahoo (d) Bing

33. LibreOffice writer में redo करने की शॉर्टकट की क्या है?
(a) Ctrl+R (b) Ctrl+Y
(c) Ctrl+Z (d) Ctrl+Shift+R

34. IP का पूर्ण रूप क्या है?
(a) Internet Protocol
(b) Including Protocol
(c) International Protocol
(d) None of the above

35. डिलीट किया हुआ ईमेल कहाँ मिलेगा?
(a) Inbox (b) Outbox
(c) Trash Mail (d) Sent Mail

36. ATM का पूर्ण रूप क्या है?
(a) Automatic Teller Machine
(b) Automated Teller Machine
(c) Automatic Transfer Money
(d) Automatic Transmission Money

37. CC का पूर्ण रूप क्या है?
(a) Carbon Copy (b) Carbon Code
(c) Character Code (d) None of the above

38. इंस्टाग्राम किससे संबंधित है?
(a) Microsoft (b) Google
(c) Facebook (d) Twitter

39. UPI में U क्या है?
(a) University (b) Unified
(c) Unique (d) Universal

40. Left Allignment कौन से Key द्वारा होता है?
(a) Ctrl+A (b) Ctrl+L
(c) Ctrl+Shift+L (d) None

41. क्लिपबोर्ड क्या है?
(a) एक प्रकार का बोर्ड
(b) हार्डवेयर
(c) कॉपी या कट किए हुए करैक्टर सेव होते हैं
(d) None of the above

42. NASSCOM का पूर्ण रूप क्या है?
(a) National Association of Software and Serving Computer
(b) National Association of Software and Server Computer
(c) National Association of Software and Service Computer
(d) None of these

43. लाइट पेन क्या है?
(a) एक तरह का पेन (b) इनपुट डिवाइस
(c) आउटपुट डिवाइस (d) इनमें से कोई नहीं

44. Bluetooth नेटवर्क होता है?
(a) LAN (b) PAN
(c) WAN (d) MAN

45. IM का पूर्ण रूप क्या है?
(a) Internet Members (b) Instant Messaging
(c) Including Media (d) None of the above

46. QR कोड बार अधिकतम डिजिट होता है?
(a) 4296 (b) 7089
(c) 2953 (d) None

47. IMEI नंबर में कितने डिजिट होते हैं?
(a) 10 (b) 12
(c) 13 (d) 15

48. CARD का पूर्ण रूप है?
(a) Cumulative Action for Rural Development
(b) Computer Aided Research and Development
(c) Center for Agriculture and Rural Development
(d) All of the above

49. OTP यूज करते हैं?
(a) सुरक्षित पैसा ट्रांसफर (b) सुरक्षित लॉगइन
(c) सुरक्षित ऑनलाइन लेनदेन (d) उपरोक्त सभी

50. ODF का पूर्ण रूप है?
(a) Old Document Format
(b) Open Document Format
(c) Open Source Document Format
(d) None of the above

51. LibreOffice शीट को Save as करने की शॉर्टकट key क्या है?
(a) Ctrl+F2 (b) Ctrl+Shift+F
(c) Ctrl+Shift+S (d) None of the above

52. QR Code यूज होता है?
(a) बैंक खाते की जानकारी
(b) किसी वेबसाइट में log in करने के लिए
(c) पैसा स्थानान्तरण करने के लिए
(d) All of the above

53. Cell मे फॉर्मूला डालने की Shortcut key है?
(a) Shift+F3 (b) Ctrl+F2
(c) Both (d) None

54. इनमे से सबसे तेज कौन सी मेमोरी एक्सेस करती है?
(a) Cache Memory (b) Register Memory
(c) Storage Memory (d) Virtual Memory

55. AI किस जनरेशन से संबंधित है?
(a) First Generation (b) Third Generation
(c) Fifth Generation (d) Sixth Generation

56. NEFT is first used in:
(a) November 2005 (b) November 2006
(c) November 2007 (d) November 2008

57. इनमे से क्या Cyber Attack है?
(a) MiTm (b) Phinishing
(c) Reply Attack (d) Wire Sniffing

58. QR Code Phone Pe में उपलब्ध होता है?
(a) True (b) False

59. .gov, .edu, .nic., are called
(a) डोमेन नेम (b) डोमेन नेम एक्सटेंशन
(c) फाइल एक्सटेंशन (d) आईपी ऐड्रेस

60. EEROM का पूर्ण रूप क्या है?
(a) Electric Erasable Read-only Memory
(b) Electronic Erasable Read-only Memory
(c) Electrically Erasable Read-only Memory
(d) None of the above

61. We can use gmail:
(a) 24*7 (b) Weekly
(c) Yearly (d) Only on Monday

62. LibreOffice Calc अधिकतम zoom नहीं कर सकते?
(a) 200 (b) 300
(c) 400 (d) 500

63. पेज ब्रेक करने की शॉर्टकट की है?
(a) Shift+Enter (b) Ctrl+Enter
(c) Enter (d) None of these

64. कौन सा नेटवर्क countries, cities, world को कनेक्ट करता है?
(a) LAN (b) WAN
(c) MAN (d) PAN

65. लिब्रे ऑफिस एक एप्लीकेशन सॉफ्टवेयर है?
(a) True (b) False

66. Solve Max where A1 to A3 range.
(a) max(A1*A3) (b) max(A1:A3)
(c) max(A1,A3) (d) max(A1-A3)

67. Find =quotient(5,2)
(a) 2 (b) 3
(c) 6 (d) 8

68. Facebook Account ओपन करने की न्यूनतम उम्र होनी चाहिए?
(a) 12 (b) 13
(c) 14 (d) 18

69. OLX क्या है?
(a) e goverence (b) e commerce
(c) e-mail (d) None

70. **कम्प्यूटर में PAN का पूर्ण रूप क्या है?**
(a) Permanent Account Number
(b) Personal Area Network
(c) Permanent Area Network
(d) None of the above

71. **Column को सिलेक्ट करने की शॉर्टकट की क्या है?**
(a) Shift+Spacebar (b) Ctrl+Spacebar
(c) Shift++ (d) Ctrl++

72. **Left Click करके सभी स्लाइड पर ले जाने से क्या होता है?**
(a) Selecting (b) Moving
(c) Dragging (d) None of the above

73. **भीम एप द्वारा अधिकतम एक दिन में कितना अमाउंट ट्रांसफर कर सकते हैं?**
(a) 10000 (b) 20000
(c) 40000 (d) 100000

74. **Phone pe क्या है?**
(a) NIC Card (b) E Wallet
(c) Messenger (d) All of the above

75. **Thesaurus के लिए शॉर्टकट की क्या है?**
(a) F7 (b) Shift+F7
(c) F5 (d) Shift+F5

76. **RDS का पूर्ण रूप क्या है?**
(a) Remote Desktop Services
(b) Remote Desktop Server
(c) Reboot Desktop Services
(d) None of the above

77. **MS Word and Writer सबसे नीचे जो दिखाई देता उसे क्या बोलते हैं?**
(a) Title Bar (b) Status Bar
(c) Task Bar (d) Menu Bar

78. **UPI PIN कितने डिजिट का होता है?**
(a) 4 (b) 6
(c) 8 (d) 4 - 6

79. **क्या आप मैसेज बिना विषय के संदेश लिखकर msg भेज सकते हैं?**
(a) True (b) False

80. **LAN MAN WAN का प्रयोग किस पीढ़ी में किया गया?**
(a) First (b) Second
(c) Third (d) Fourth

81. **IC का निर्माण किसने किया?**
(a) बिल गेट्स (b) जैक किल्बी
(c) मार्क एंडरसन (d) हरमन हेलोरीत

82. **LibreOffice Writer में प्रिंट प्रीव्यू की शॉर्टकट की क्या है?**
(a) Ctrl+P (b) Ctrl+F2
(c) Ctrl+Shift+P (d) Ctrl+Shift+O

83. **UTR का पूर्ण रूप क्या है?**
(a) Unique Transaction Reference
(b) Unique Transfer Reference
(c) Uniquely Transaction Reference
(d) None of the above

84. **ULSI, LSI, VLSI का प्रयोग किस पीढ़ी में किया गया?**
(a) First (b) Second
(c) Third (d) Fourth

85. **LibreOffie में पेज ब्रेक की कमांड किस मेन्यू में मिलती है?**
(a) File (b) Insert
(c) Format (d) Tools

86. **LibreOffie में ग्रिड लाइन्स को इन्सर्ट किया जा सकता है?**
(a) True (b) False

87. **इंटरनेट का उपयोग कर आप कर सकते हैं?**
(a) ऑनलाइन टीवी देखना
(b) ऑनलाइन गाने लोड करना
(c) ऑनलाइन मोबाइल फोन खरीदना
(d) उपरोक्त सभी

88. **बैंक किस पर ब्याज लेता है?**
(a) ऋणों पर (b) जमाओं पर
(c) दोनों (d) इनमें से कोई नहीं

89. **निम्न में कौन सा बैंक खाते का एक प्रकार नहीं है?**
(a) चालू खाता (b) बचत खाता
(c) चिट फंड खाता (d) आवर्ती जमा खाता

90. **वह क्या शब्द है जो आमतौर पर वेब पेज पर रेखांकित प्रदर्शित होता है?**
(a) एक हाइपरलिंक (b) एक वेब पता
(c) एक महत्वपूर्ण वर्ड (d) एक सक्रिय शब्द

91. **विषम क्या है?**
(a) POP (b) SMT
(c) FTP (d) IMAP

92. **एक ब्राउजर?**
(a) वेब साइट बताने का प्रोग्राम है
(b) इंटरनेट से कनेक्ट करने वाला प्रोग्राम है
(c) वेब पर वेबसाइट देखने में प्रयोग किये जाने वाला प्रोग्राम है
(d) उपरोक्त सभी

93. **नोटपैड फाइल का डिफाल्ट फाइल एक्सटेंशन है?**
(a) .txt (b) .npd

(c) .rtf (d) None of these

94. LibreOffice Writer में सेव की गई फाइल के साथ कौन सा एक्सटेंशन जुड़ा होता है?

(a) .lbr (b) .doc

(c) .odt (d) .wrt

95. एक प्रोग्राम जो आपके द्वारा लिखे हुए डॉक्यूमेंट्स बनाने में और आवश्यकता पड़ने पर उसमे वापस जाकर संशोधन करने में सहायता करता है?

(a) Tool Bar (b) Folder

(c) Home Row Key (d) Word Processor

96. LibreOffice Calc में सेव की गयी फाइल के साथ कौन सा एक्स्टेंशन जुड़ा होता है?

(a) .dos (b) .ods

(c) .lst (d) .wrt

97. LibreOffice Impress में सेव की गई फाइल के साथ कौन कौन सा एक्स्टेंशन जुड़ा होता है?

(a) .lst (b) .wrt

(c) .odp (d) .ods

98. LibreOffice Impress में Macros की कमाण्ड किस मेन्यू में मिलती है?

(a) Slide (b) Tools

(c) Insert (d) View

99. LibreOffice Writer में Super Script की शॉर्टकट की है?

(a) Ctrl+Shift+S (b) Ctrl+Shift+P

(c) Ctrl+Alt+P (d) None

100. LibreOffice Writer में Sub Script की शॉर्टकट की है?

(a) Ctrl+Shift+B (b) Ctrl+Shift+S

(c) Ctrl+Alt+P (d) Ctrl+Shift+P

Answers

1.	(b)	2.	(c)	3.	(a)	4.	(b)
5.	(b)	6.	(c)	7.	(c)	8.	(a)
9.	(b)	10.	(a)	11.	(c)	12.	(d)
13.	(b)	14.	(b)	15.	(c)	16.	(c)
17.	(b)	18.	(a)	19.	(a)	20.	(a)
21.	(b)	22.	(b)	23.	(a)	24.	(a)
25.	(d)	26.	(a)	27.	(b)	28.	(a)
29.	(a)	30.	(d)	31.	(a)	32.	(a)
33.	(b)	34.	(a)	35.	(a)	36.	(b)
37.	(c)	38.	(c)	39.	(b)	40.	(b)
41.	(c)	42.	(c)	43.	(b)	44.	(b)
45.	(b)	46.	(b)	47.	(d)	48.	(b)
49.	(d)	50.	(b)	51.	(b)	52.	(d)
53.	(c)	54.	(a)	55.	(c)	56.	(a)
57.	(a)	58.	(a)	59.	(b)	60.	(a)
61	(a)	62.	(d)	63.	(b)	64.	(b)
65.	(a)	66.	(b)	67.	(a)	68.	(b)
69.	(b)	70.	(b)	71.	(a)	72.	(b)
73.	(c)	74.	(b)	75.	(b)	76.	(a)
77.	(b)	78.	(d)	79.	(a)	80.	(d)
81.	(b)	82.	(d)	83.	(a)	84.	(d)
85.	(b)	86.	(a)	87.	(d)	88.	(a)
89.	(c)	90.	(a)	91.	(c)	92.	(c)
93.	(a)	94.	(c)	95.	(d)	96.	(b)
97.	(c)	98.	(b)	99.	(b)	100.	(a)

Model Test Paper VI

1. **Twisted-pair network cable uses which RJ connector?**
   (a) RJ-14 (b) RJ-15
   (c) RJ-45 (d) RJ-25
2. **If you see a paperclip icon next to a message in the message list, that means....**
   (a) Message is of high periority
   (b) Message is time sensitive
   (c) Message has an attachment
   (d) Message has been read
3. **Which of the printer is used in conjunction with computers uses dry ink powder?**
   (a) Line Printer (b) Daisy Wheel Printer
   (c) Laser Printer (d) Dot Matrix Printer
4. **By encryption of a text we mean:**
   (a) Expanding it
   (b) Compressing it
   (c) Hashing it
   (d) Scrambling it to preserve its security
5. **OS does not boot itself when a system is**
   (a) Reset (b) Shutdown
   (c) Restart (d) Power On
6. **A software which supports the basic functions computer usage and helps to run the computer hardware is:**
   (a) Operating System (b) Printer
   (c) Registers (d) Control Unit
7. **In MS-Excel 2013, a worksheet can have a maximum of .... number of rows.**
   (a) 1024576 (b) 32000
   (c) 1048576 (d) 256
8. **How can you stop a slide show?**
   (a) By pressing left arrow key
   (b) By pressing Esc key
   (c) By pressing up arrow key
   (d) By pressing down arrow key
9. **Which of these domain is restricted to commercial purpose?**
   (a) .org (b) .com
   (c) .edi (d) .net
10. **......... is required when more than one person uses a central computer at the same time.**
    (a) Mouse (b) Terminal
    (c) Digitizer (d) Light Pen
11. **Does the use of RPA tools is interfere with underlying computer systems?**
    (a) No (b) Yes
    (c) No Idea (d) Undecided
12. **Which one is not an element of IoT?**
    (a) Process (b) People
    (c) Things (d) Security
13. **Which of the following is not an example of hardware?**
    (a) Printer (b) Scanner
    (c) Mouse (d) Interpreter
14. **Which symbol must for all formula begin with?**
    (a) * (b) =
    (c) @ (d) &
15. **A dial up connection to the internet:**
    (a) Grand permission for exchanging data between end-poinds
    (b) A connection found often in house
    (c) A good expert medium connect with LAN
    (d) Both (B) and (C)
16. **Which of the following view is not one of Power Point view?**
    (a) Normal view (b) Slide sorter view
    (c) Sorter view (d) Slide view
17. **When you link data maintained in a excel work book to a work document.**
    (a) The word document must contain a hyperlink
    (b) The word document contains a reference to the original source application
    (c) The word document can not be edited
    (d) The word document contains a copy of the actual data
18. **Which of the following memories allows simultaneous read and writes operations?**
    (a) RAM (b) ROM
    (c) EPROM (d) None of these
19. **Which command is used to change the file name?**
    (a) Rename (b) Ren
    (c) Both as above (d) None of these
20. **A double sided magnetic disk pack that has six disks normally uses .... surfaces for this pack.**

(a) 12 (b) 10
(c) 9 (d) 6

21. Internet is ....
(a) De centralized system
(b) Complex system
(c) Dynamic system
(d) All of the above

22. Which of the following memories has the shortest access times?
(a) Magneti Bubble Memory
(b) Cache Memory
(c) RAM
(d) Magnegic Core Memory

23. The bounce mail is...............
(a) Junk mail
(b) Mallware attack
(c) Mail delevery information
(d) Informatic mail of wrong email

24. If you receive an email message that includes multiple recipients, and you wish to respond back to the same list of recipients, use the .... comand
(a) Forward all (b) Forward
(c) Reply all (d) Reply

25. In ASCII .... characters can be created.
(a) 1024 (b) 128
(c) 255 (d) 256

26. .... is program designed to destroy data on your computer and can travel to "infect" other computer.
(a) Torpedo (b) Virus
(c) Disease (d) Hurrican

27. You can edit existing Excel data by pressing:
(a) F3 key (b) F1 key
(c) F2 key (d) F4 key

28. The following is a slide transition effect:
(a) Dissolve (b) Wipe all over
(c) Bit by Bit (d) None of the above

29. What is the shortcut key to open start menu?
(a) Ctrl+Esc
(b) Express windows key
(c) Both (A) and (B)
(d) None of these

30. Aadhar is
(a) Identity certificate issued by UIDAI
(b) A 12 digit card
(c) Both (a) and (b)
(d) None of the above

31. Which of the following is an example of system software?
(a) Loader (b) Operating System
(c) Linker (d) All of these

32. The speed of a dot matrix printer is measured in ....
(a) Pages per second'
(b) Pages per minute
(c) Character per second
(d) Character per minute

33. Internet traffic is also known as
(a) Concession (b) Confession
(c) Concatenation (d) Congestion

34. The email address of the recipient of your mail is written in
(a) From (b) To
(c) BCC (d) CC

35. This is the menu command to create a text box on a slide:
(a) View/text box (b) Tool/text box
(c) Format/text box (d) Insert/text box

36. Computers use the .... number system to store data and perform calculations.
(a) Octal (b) Binary
(c) Hexadecimal (d) Decimal

37. In which year, National e-Governance plan(NeGP) was launched?
(a) 18 May, 2006 (b) 10 May, 2006
(c) 15 August, 2010 (d) None of these

38. Which of the device does not work as both input and output device?
(a) Light Pen (b) Modem
(c) Mouse (d) CD Rom

39. Within how much time the entire Internet Ticketing System concept was conceived, formulated and implemented by IRCTC?
(a) 6 Months (b) 5 Months
(c) 10 Months (d) 9 Months

40. Special effects used to introduce slides in a presentation are called.
(a) Effects (b) Current Animation
(c) Custome Animation (d) Change

41. The hexadecimal number system consists of the following symbols ....
(a) 0-9 (b) 0-7

(c) 0-9, A-F (d) None of these

42. e-Hospitals of Digital Health has been promoted by
(a) Ministry of External Affairs
(b) Ministry of Home Affairs
(c) Ministry of Agriculture
(d) Ministry of Health of Family Welfare?

43. Which of the following form, data is stored in computer?
(a) Binary (b) Decimal
(c) Octal (d) Hexadecimal

44. Which WAN connection technology uses high-connections made over regular analog phone lines?
(a) Cellular (b) Cable
(c) VPN (d) D.S.I.

45. What is the base/Radix of hexadecimal number?
(a) 8 (b) 2
(c) 10 (d) 16

46. A telephone number, a birth date, and a customer name are all examples of.......
(a) A database (b) A file
(c) A record (d) Data

47. CC in the email stand for:
(a) Carbon Copy (b) Create Copy
(c) Cyber Copy (d) None of these

48. Outlook express is a ....
(a) Search Engine (b) Browsers
(c) E-mail client (d) Editor

49. .... number system is usually followed in a typical 32-bit computer.
(a) Hexadecimal (b) Decimal
(c) Octal (d) Binary

50. DNS in internet technology stands for ....
(a) Domain Name System
(b) Dynamic Name System
(c) Distributed Name System
(d) None of the above

51. Statistical operations are not allowed in excel.
(a) True (b) False

52. ISDN is an example of circuit switched network.
(a) True (b) False

53. M.S. Excess is most popular business oriented social networking site.
(a) True (b) False

54. The back and forward keys can be used to visit only page, from the similar websites.
(a) True (b) False

55. Bullets and Numbering appears in the standard toolbar
(a) True (b) False

56. Windows menu allows you to work with two documents simulatenously.
(a) True (b) False

57. M.S. Excel ignores manual page breaks when you use the fit to option of the page setup
(a) True (b) False

58. In the private Filtering helps prevent the websites you go to from automatically sharing details about your visit with the third party content provider websites.
(a) True (b) False

59. Pressing Esc button during the slide show ends the presentation.
(a) True (b) False

60. Notepad is a text editor
(a) True (b) False

61. POS is a digital device.
(a) True (b) False

62. To arrange your bookmarks menu into sections and separators.
(a) True (b) False

63. Search engine maintains the keywords and URL of the heavy database.
(a) True (b) False

64. In Excel, if user writes = 6+7x9, , then the result comes as 69.
(a) True (b) False

65. A footnote is printed at the bottom of each page.
(a) True (b) False

66. FTP is the short form of File Transaction Protocol.
(a) True (b) False

67. In M.S. Dos, CD command shows the file and folder of any directory.
(a) True (b) False

68. VDU (Visual Display Unit) is used for input and output devices both.
(a) True (b) False

69. .dot extension is used for word template.
(a) True (b) False

70. The two parts of any email combined by the symbol @.
    (a) True (b) False
71. 'A' is a primary hard disk drive in window operating system.
    (a) True (b) False
72. SUM( ) function contains more than 30 arguments.
    (a) True (b) False
73. Window 2003 server is an operating system.
    (a) True (b) False
74. In business-to-consumers (B2C), a business sells to a business but delivers the product or servie to an individual consumer.
    (a) True (b) False
75. Operating system manage the monitor and printer.
    (a) True (b) False
76. X.25 is an example of packet switched network.
    (a) True (b) False
77. Bold characters are little bulky than normal characters.
    (a) True (b) False
78. Editing is not possible in print preview of word document.
    (a) True (b) False
79. Can users access state-wise department services on UMANG,
    (a) True (b) False
80. Email address are case-sensitive.
    (a) True (b) False
81. When you create formula that contins a function, the insert function dialog box helps you to enter worksheet functions.
    (a) True (b) False
82. Peer-to-peer networking refers a central server by which all computers of the network connect directly.
    (a) True (b) False
83. ALU is a part of CPU.
    (a) True (b) False
84. Two persons can have the same email address.
    (a) True (b) False
85. Multiple series is introduce by the help of pi charts.
    (a) True (b) False
86. You can't copy or move worksheet from a workbook to another workbook.
    (a) True (b) False
87. Function key F5 is used for showing the slide show in power point presentation.
    (a) True (b) False
88. Does RPA software's can be used for software testing?
    (a) True (b) False
89. .wav and mid files are two types of sound that can be added in the presentation.
    (a) True (b) False
90. Scripting language cannot be disabled in browser.
    (a) True (b) False
91. Program or instruction that tells the computer what to do is termed as hardware.
    (a) True (b) False
92. System bus is used for connecting CPU and central switch.
    (a) True (b) False
93. Webpages download from websites can store in your computer.
    (a) True (b) False
94. Blockchain is the same as bitcoin.
    (a) True (b) False
95. Print button on the standard toolbar will print the entire document by using the default setting.
    (a) True (b) False
96. The Auto Content wizard creates the structure and contents based on the choices you make.
    (a) True (b) False
97. [Ctrl+F] shortcut key acts the similar operation in M.S. Word and Excel.
    (a) True (b) False
98. Align the text is similar as indenting the text.
    (a) True (b) False
99. Information is carried in data communication thousands of kilometers.
    (a) True (b) False
100. Primary memory contains more storage capacity than secondary memory.
    (a) True (b) False

Answers

1.	(c)	2.	(c)	3.	(c)	4.	(d)
5.	(b)	6.	(a)	7.	(d)	8.	(a)

9.	(b)	10.	(b)	11.	(a)	12.	(d)
13.	(d)	14.	(b)	15.	(b)	16.	(c)
17.	(b)	18.	(a)	19.	(c)	20.	(b)
21.	(d)	22.	(b)	23.	(d)	24.	(b)
25.	(b)	26.	(c)	27.	(c)	28.	(a)
29.	(c)	30.	(d)	31.	(d)	32.	(c)
33.	(d)	34.	(b)	35.	(d)	36.	(b)
37.	(a)	38.	(c)	39.	(d)	40.	(b)
41.	(c)	42.	(d)	43.	(a)	44.	(d)
45.	(b)	46.	(c)	47.	(a)	48.	(c)
49.	(d)	50.	(a)	51.	(b)	52.	(a)
53.	(b)	54.	(b)	55.	(a)	56.	(a)
57.	(a)	58.	(a)	59.	(a)	60.	(a)
61	(a)	62.	(a)	63.	(a)	64.	(a)
65.	(a)	66.	(b)	67.	(b)	68.	(a)
69.	(a)	70.	(a)	71.	(b)	72.	(a)
73.	(a)	74.	(b)	75.	(a)	76.	(a)
77.	(a)	78.	(a)	79.	(a)	80.	(a)
81.	(a)	82.	(b)	83.	(a)	84.	(b)
85.	(a)	86.	(b)	87.	(a)	88.	(a)
89.	(a)	90.	(b)	91.	(b)	92.	(a)
93.	(a)	94.	(b)	95.	(a)	96.	(a)
97.	(a)	98.	(b)	99.	(a)	100.	(b)

Model Test Paper VII

1. **Un soliticited commercial email is known as ....**
   (a) Malware (b) Spam
   (c) Spyware (d) Virus

2. **GUI is used as an interface between ....**
   (a) Human and Machine
   (b) Hardware and Software
   (c) Software and User
   (d) None of the above

3. **What is the shortcut key for new document a presentation from the beginning?**
   (a) Alt+N (b) F5
   (c) Shift+F5 (d) Ctrl+F5

4. **The .... field is a counter used to limit packed lifetimes.**
   (a) Length (b) Fragement offset
   (c) Time to live (d) Versions

5. **The diameter of fibre optic cable expressed in which measurement?**
   (a) microns (b) cm
   (c) ohm (d) mm

6. **In MS Word, the backspace key:**
   (a) Erase the character at the place of cursor
   (b) Erase the character left to the cursor
   (c) Erase a word
   (d) Erase the character right to the cursor

7. **What cannot be done from windows control panel?**
   (a) Printer configuration
   (b) Run application
   (c) Install an application
   (d) Add fonts

8. **The formula that will add the value of cell D4 to the value of C2 and then multiply by the value in B2 is...**
   (a) D+C2*B2 (b) (D4+C2)*B2
   (c) [(B2*(D4+C2)] (d) =(D4+C2)*B2

9. **A(n) .... search is a search whose hits are restricted to Web pages within the current Web site.**
   (a) Exploratory (b) Hierarchical
   (c) Site (d) Global

10. **Inventor of Email system?**
    (a) Zukerberg (b) Alan Turin
    (c) Ray Tomilson (d) Wint Cerf

11. **Shortcut key to insert a hyperlink in a slide**
    (a) Ctrl+K (b) Ctrl+H
    (c) Ctrl+D (d) Hyperlink insert

12. **For which of the following task MS Word is not best suited?**
    (a) Prepare slides to show in workshop or similar
    (b) Combine main document and data source for sending letter to many users
    (c) For writing of 100 pages letter
    (d) For autoformat of existing document

13. **Output of the excel expression '=64/8/2'**
    (a) 8 (b) 4
    (c) 32 (d) 16

14. **Which of the following is a GRAPHICAL PACKAGE?**
    (a) MS Excel (b) Corel Draw
    (c) MS Word (d) None of these

15. **While selecting the documents in MS Word keystroke + Homes will move the insertion point to........**
    (a) Right to a word
    (b) No effect
    (c) Beginning of the row
    (d) End of the row

16. **A function in MS Excel is........**
    (a) For case and complex calculations
    (b) A readymade formula
    (c) Start with '$' symbol
    (d) None of the above

17. **Rout redistribution is the process of introducing external routes into an .... network.**
    (a) BGP (b) EGP
    (c) Hybrid (d) OSPF

18. **Who was the founder of Bluetooth?**
    (a) Martin Cooper (b) Ericson
    (c) Apple (d) Steve Jobs

19. **Which of them is software used for 3D printing?**
    (a) Corel Draw (b) Auto CAD
    (c) Cura (d) Adobe Photoshop

20. **The two kinds of main memory are:**
    (a) Random and Sequential
    (b) Primary and Secondary

(c) ROM and RAM
(d) All of the these

21. MIME stand for
(a) Multipurpose Internet Mail Email
(b) Multipurpose Internet Mail Extensions
(c) Multipurpose International Mail End
(d) Multipurpose International Mail Entity

22. Which key cannot be used to enter data in a cell of Excel sheet?
(a) Enter key (b) Arrow key
(c) Tab key (d) Esc key

23. Which device is used as the standard pointing device in a Graphical User Environment?
(a) Mouse (b) Keyboard
(c) Track Ball (d) Joystick

24. The software used to view web pages on the WWW is ....
(a) Web browser (b) Web reader
(c) Web server (d) None of these

25. Change case command appear in .... menu.
(a) Insert (b) Tool
(c) Edit (d) Format

26. How many bits are there in the IPV4 address?
(a) 5 bits (b) 16 bits
(c) 32 bits (d) 64 bits

27. What is the maximum zoom percentage in Microsoft Power Point?
(a) 400% (b) 300%
(c) 200% (d) 100%

28. In SMTP the command to write receivers mail address is written with this command.
(a) Rcpt to (b) Send to
(c) Mail to
(d) None of the mentioned

29. The Recycle Bin is configured automatically to be able to store files equal to ....
(a) 15% (b) 10%
(c) 5% (d) 1%

30. Where can you buy cryptocurrency?
(a) An exchange
(b) A private transaction
(c) A bitcoin
(d) All of the above

31. Formatting of a block of text can be cleared by ....
(a) Selection of the AutoFormat
(b) Right click on mouse
(c) Ctrl+F
(d) Use of Edit-clear Format

32. What is e-commerce normally associated with?
(a) Buy and Selling (b) Watching Videos
(c) Reviewing Product (d) Making Friends

33. Full for of WORM is?
(a) Write on Random Memory
(b) Write Once Read Memory
(c) Work On Reak Memory
(d) None

34. Which of the following should you use if you want all the slide in the presentation to have the same look?
(a) Outline view
(b) Slide Layout option
(c) Add a slide option
(d) Presentation design template

35. When applying a design to a presentation, thumbnails of the available design templates are displayed in this section of the pane.
(a) Design templae (b) Outline
(c) Slide (d) Available for use

36. Which particular generation of computers is associated with artificial intelligence?
(a) Second (b) Third
(c) Fourth (d) Fifth

37. You can logged in remote computer through.
(a) Using FTP (b) Using Telnet
(c) Using HTTP (d) None of the above

38. Which one is not found in Window Accessories?
(a) Notpad (b) Wordpad
(c) Internet Explorer (d) Paint Brush

39. Which layer of International Standard Organization OSI model is responsible for creating and recognizing frame boundaries?
(a) Physical layer (b) Data link layer
(c) Network layer (d) Transport layer

40. In Excel, when numbers are typed inside a cell, the default alignment is
(a) Center align (b) Left align
(c) Justify (d) Right align

41. POS stand for
(a) Permanent Server (b) Point of Service
(c) Point of Sale (d) Partition of Server

42. ATM means:
(a) Auto Truck of Mahindra
(b) Any Time Money
(c) Automated Teller Machine
(d) None of the above

43. Aadhar card is issued by:
(a) By Income Tax Department
(b) By Bank
(c) By Municipal Corporation
(d) By UIDAI

44. Computer system consists of......
(a) Software (b) Hardware
(c) Both (a) and (b) (d) None

45. Which of the following is the software used for document collaboration?
(a) Microsoft Project (b) Microsoft Excel
(c) Group Office (d) Microsoft Word

46. External devices such as printers, keyboard and modems are known as:
(a) Peripherals
(b) Addon Devices
(c) Additional Hardware Devices
(d) P Extension Slot Add-on

47. For a broswer to connect to other resources, the location or address of the resources must be specified. There addresses are called:
(a) Packets (b) E-mail forms
(c) MSN (d) URLs

48. Which of the following is not a view of MS PowerPoint.
(a) Slideshow view (b) Slide view
(c) Presentation view (d) Outline view

49. The act of writing a post for a blog is called:
(a) Blogger (b) Blog
(c) Blogosphere (d) Blogging

50. Personal computer use a number of chips mounted on a main circuit bord. What is the common name for such boards?
(a) Motherboard (b) Ethernet
(c) Green board (d) Red board

51. On pressing the Home button, the active cell reaches at the column A in the current row.
(a) True (b) False

52. To start the pine program, select the option from the menu by pressing <L> + Enter.
(a) True (b) False

53. Ctrl+J shortcut key is used to print a part of excel worksheet.
(a) True (b) False

54. To reach at the last cell where the content has been written, we use [Ctrl+End] command.
(a) True (b) False

55. The distance from the top of the page to your insertion point is displayed in the status bar of the document.
(a) True (b) False

56. Styles can be used to generate a table contents quickly in word.
(a) True (b) False

57. HTML is used for creating home page on the World Wide Web.
(a) True (b) False

58. FTP is a client server program to retrieve the document.
(a) True (b) False

59. From the Mail Merge Helper dialog box, you can only open an existing data sourcing but cannot create.
(a) True (b) False

60. GUI operating system is much easier to learn and to use for the user since there is no need to learn the command for it.
(a) True (b) False

61. Length( ) function is used for finding the length of string in cell.
(a) True (b) False

62. Copying file from one computer to other on internet is called downloading.
(a) True (b) False

63. In Email client program, by which method you can filter the A-Z, just click on header and filter such messages.
(a) True (b) False

64. [Ctrl+;] is used for inserting the current date in the active cell.
(a) True (b) False

65. ISP is the short form Internet Source Provider.
(a) True (b) False

66. In dial-up connection, you can connect your computer to ISP server with the help of modem.
(a) True (b) False

67. **In 1991, Linux Torveld inroduced the Linux operating system.**
(a) True (b) False

68. **Blog is a website where the entries are made in journal style and displayed in reverse chronological order.**
(a) True (b) False

69. **The first page of website is called home page.**
(a) True (b) False

70. **DNS provides the mapping of IP with domain name.**
(a) True (b) False

71. **PowerPoint contains more than 24 layouts.**
(a) True (b) False

72. **Cookies store the information of webpages in your favorite list.**
(a) True (b) False

73. **You cannot change font style of entire workbook from a single command. It can be changed only on worksheet level.**
(a) True (b) False

74. **The [Shift+Tab] shortcut key moves the mouse pointer to the next cell in word table.**
(a) True (b) False

75. **Example of social network are Facebook, Twitter etc.**
(a) True (b) False

76. **The auto fit feature to contents enables word to widen on narrow columns based on the contents you insert in table.**
(a) True (b) False

77. **Word template does not include style formatting.**
(a) True (b) False

78. **SMTP was introduced to manage offline mails.**
(a) True (b) False

79. **The same header is necessarily printed on all even pages of the document.**
(a) True (b) False

80. **The instructions of program execution are indentified by Control Unit.**
(a) True (b) False

81. **You insert manual page break when you want to force a page break when you want to force a page break.**
(a) True (b) False

82. **In word, Ctrl+U can underline the selected text.**
(a) True (b) False

83. **Sum( ) functions offer you the possibility to view different results depending on the entered condition:**
(a) True (b) False

84. **Email component of internet explorer is called outlook express**
(a) True (b) False

85. **MIME defines mechanisms for sending other kinds of information in email like any file image, sounds, movies and computer program.**
(a) True (b) False

86. **The use of email is for sending the broadcast message, but only in a company.**
(a) True (b) False

87. **When we copy the formula in excel, absolute value change doesn't change.**
(a) True (b) False

88. **Immersive virtual reality is the most expensive form of VR.**
(a) True (b) False

89. **MS Word supports at most 500% zooming.**
(a) True (b) False

90. **Email is responsible for sending message based on text.**
(a) True (b) False

91. **MTA stand for Mail Transfer Agent.**
(a) True (b) False

92. **When any formatted number doesn't fit in the active cell then it displays by ####**
(a) True (b) False

93. **OSI model used for data transmission.**
(a) True (b) False

94. **Big online business website like Flipkart, Snapdeal uses Facebook or Gmail data to view the customers information or behavior.**
(a) True (b) False

95. **IMAP stands for Internet Message Access Protocol.**
(a) True (b) False

96. **The current date cannot be inserted in the header section.**
(a) True (b) False

97. **Left key of the mouse is use to open the pop-up menu.**
(a) True (b) False

98. You should never promote your business offline.

(a) True (b) False

99. Mostly word processors have maxmum size of a page as 22 inch x 22 inch.

(a) True (b) False

100. Telnet service enables the internet user to login in other computer from personal computer on the internet.

(a) True (b) False

Answers

1.	(b)	2.	(c)	3.	(a)	4.	(c)
5.	(a)	6.	(b)	7.	(b)	8.	(d)
9.	(c)	10.	(c)	11.	(a)	12.	(a)
13.	(d)	14.	(b)	15.	(c)	16.	(b)
17.	(d)	18.	(b)	19.	(c)	20.	(c)
21.	(b)	22.	(d)	23.	(b)	24.	(a)
25.	(d)	26.	(a)	27.	(a)	28.	(a)
29.	(c)	30.	(d)	31.	(d)	32.	(a)
33.	(b)	34.	(d)	35.	(a)	36.	(d)
37.	(b)	38.	(c)	39.	(d)	40.	(d)
41.	(c)	42.	(c)	43.	(d)	44.	(c)
45.	(c)	46.	(a)	47.	(d)	48.	(c)
49.	(d)	50.	(a)	51.	(a)	52.	(a)
53.	(b)	54.	(a)	55.	(a)	56.	(a)
57.	(a)	58.	(a)	59.	(b)	60.	(a)
61	(b)	62.	(a)	63.	(a)	64.	(a)
65.	(b)	66.	(a)	67.	(a)	68.	(a)
69.	(a)	70.	(a)	71.	(a)	72.	(a)
73.	(a)	74.	(b)	75.	(a)	76.	(a)
77.	(b)	78.	(b)	79.	(a)	80.	(a)
81.	(a)	82.	(a)	83.	(b)	84.	(a)
85.	(a)	86.	(b)	87.	(a)	88.	(a)
89.	(a)	90.	(b)	91.	(a)	92.	(a)
93.	(a)	94.	(a)	95.	(a)	96.	(b)
97.	(b)	98.	(b)	99.	(a)	100.	(a)

Model Test Paper VIII

1. **A DVD is an example of a**
   (a) Output Devices (b) Hard Disk
   (c) SSSD (d) Optical Device

2. **A file without extension is ..... in MS DOS.**
   (a) executive file (b) Not recognizable
   (c) a doc file (d) database file

3. **Which of the following is not windows e-mail programme?**
   (a) Outlook (b) Eudora
   (c) Pegasus (d) Pine

4. **The application of smart TVs is............**
   (a) Internet of Things
   (b) Not internet of things
   (c) Can't say (d) None of these

5. **Maximum number of handouts in one page are:**
   (a) 20 (b) 9
   (c) 12 (d) 6

6. **"Accidently, you made a mistake when working with your document. How can you undo that action?"**
   (a) Ctrl+Y (b) Ctrl+X
   (c) Ctrl+U (d) Ctrl+Z

7. **ISDN stands for.....**
   (a) International Subscriber Dialup Networks
   (b) Integral Service Dynamic Network
   (c) Integrated Service Digital Network
   (d) International Service Digital Network

8. **What is the name of the bar normally displayed across the bottom to the windows screen which holds the Start Menu?**
   (a) Status Bar (b) Title Bar
   (c) Task Bar (d) Horizontal Bar

9. **Simple Mail Transfer Protocol (SMTP) utilizes .... as the transport layer protocol for electronic mail transfer.**
   (a) UDP (b) TCP
   (c) SCTP (d) DCCP

10. **Under which menu, page setup appears.**
    (a) File Menu (b) Tools Menu
    (c) Slideshow Menu (d) None of these

11. **A .... is an additional set of commands that the computer displays after you make a selection from the main menu.**
    (a) Sub-menu (b) Dialog-box
    (c) Menu Selection (d) All of these

12. **In powerpoint, which shortcut key is used to insert a new slide?**
    (a) Ctrl+N (b) Ctrl+M
    (c) Ctrl+K (d) Ctrl+D

13. **The file type .... indicates the file is a Word document.**
    (a) .wor (b) .doc
    (c) .msw (d) .wrd

14. **Graphic objects can be inserted into word through ....**
    (a) Frame file (b) ClipArt
    (c) Chart (d) All of these

15. **The operating system for a computer does the following.**
    (a) Manages computer resources
    (b) Manages disk and file
    (c) Manages computer memory
    (d) All of above

16. **Which command is used to copy files?**
    (a) Discopy (b) Copy
    (c) Ctrl+C (d) All of these

17. **The Horizontal and Vertical lines on the worksheet are called ....**
    (a) Grid line (b) Sheet line
    (c) Crosshair (d) Block line

18. **SMTP is used to deliver messages to:**
    (a) Users mailbox (b) Users terminal
    (c) Both (a) and (b) (d) None of the above

19. **At what point will VR displays the indistinguishable from reality?**
    (a) 12 k resolution (b) 8k resolution
    (c) 20k resolutin (d) 16k resolution

20. **The .... protocol has features that allow uploading of mail messages.**
    (a) IMAP (b) SNMP
    (c) HTTP (d) POP3

21. **The combination of the column letter and row number for a cell in an Excel worksheet is called.**
    (a) Cell indentification number
    (b) Cell across

(c) Cell Indentify (d) Cell reference

22. **We can delete the maximum number of e-mail at a time is**
(a) Only two (b) Multiple
(c) Only three (d) Only one

23. **Expansion of SMTP is**
(a) Simple Message Transfer Protocol
(b) Simple Mail Transfer Protocol
(c) Simple Message Transmission Protocol
(d) Simple Mail Transmission Protocol

24. **The communication protocol used by Internet is:**
(a) TELNET (b) HTTP
(c) FTP (d) UTP

25. **Port number for SMTP protocol is ....**
(a) 25 (b) 22
(c) 80 (d) 110

26. **Which of the following keyboard shortcuts is used to exit word?**
(a) Alt+F4 (b) Ctrl+F4
(c) Ctrl+W (d) Ctrl+E

27. **The PowerPoint wizard includes ....**
(a) AutoContent wizard
(b) AutoContent and pick a toll wizard
(c) Pick a tool wizard
(d) Chart wizard and AutoContent wizard

28. **Short cut to open file in LibreOffice writed is:**
(a) Ctrl+A (b) Ctrl+O
(c) Ctrl+Z (d) Ctrl+F

29. **What is the maximum length allowed for primary name of a computer file under DOS?**
(a) 3 (b) 6
(c) 8 (d) 12

30. **Magnetic tape can be served as:**
(a) Output media
(b) Secondary storage device
(c) Input media
(d) All of the above

31. **Formatting toolbar has lot of buttons that you can quickly apply to numerical data on the worksheet. These buttons are:**
(a) Percent style (b) Currency style
(c) Comma style (d) All of these

32. **Which of the following is a word processing software?**
(a) MS Word (b) Word Perfect
(c) Easy Word (d) All of these

33. **You use .... in yours slide to hold text, clip art, and charts.**
(a) Drowing box (b) Textbox
(c) Window (d) Placeholder

34. **In which year NEFT services has been started?**
(a) 2002 (b) 2005
(c) 1999 (d) 2009

35. **Four your E-mail, PGP allows you to**
(a) Encrypt (b) Enhance
(c) Design (d) Decrypt

36. **Which of the following protocols is used by internet mail?**
(a) TCP/IP (b) HTTP
(c) FTP (d) None

37. **PAN card is valid only for:**
(a) Address of card holders
(b) ID of card holders
(c) Date of birth of card holders
(d) All of the above

38. **The paper orientation for printing is:**
(a) Landscape (b) Potrait
(c) Both (a) and (b) (d) None of the above

39. **What is meaning of EEPROM?**
(a) Electrically Erasable Programmable
(b) Electronically Erasable Programmable Read Only Memory
(c) Electronically Erasable Programmable Reach Only Memory
(d) Electrically Erasable Programmable Ready Only Memory

40. **The personal computer industry was started by**
(a) Apple (b) IBM
(c) HCL (d) Compaq

41. **The secondary storage devices can only store data but they cannot parform:**
(a) Logic operations
(b) Airthmetic operations
(c) Fetch operations
(d) None of the above

42. **Which mobile wallet does not permit cash withdrawl.**
(a) Semi-open wallet (b) Open wallet
(c) Semi-close wallet (d) None of the above

43. Name is a device that changes information into digital form?
(a) Open wallet (b) Semi-closed wallet
(c) Semi-open wallet (d) None of these

44. As compare to the secondary memory the primary memory of a computer is.
(a) Cheap (b) Large
(c) Idle (d) Fast

45. What type of device is 3.5 inch floppy drive?
(a) Storage (b) Input
(c) Output (d) Software

46. The underline and centre button can be found on the .... toolbar.
(a) Outline (b) Drawing
(c) Formatting (d) Standard

47. Data processing performed by several separate computers/computer networks at several different location, linked by a communication facility is known as.
(a) Centralized Processing
(b) Distributed Resources
(c) Online Resources
(d) Batch Processing

48. Which type of storage devices is a BIOS?
(a) Secondary (b) Primary
(c) Tertiary (d) None of the above

49. When sendin an email, the line describes the contents of the message.
(a) To (b) Contents
(c) CC (d) Subject

50. A bit of the text which is automatically inserted at the bottom of every sent message is known as:
(a) Signature
(b) Personal level indicator
(c) People text
(d) People widget

51. UFS is the short form of Unix File System.
(a) True (b) False

52. ALU contains CPU, memory board, device boards, power plug, etc.
(a) True (b) False

53. Bullets and numbering appears in view menu in power point.
(a) True (b) False

54. To name a constant, you use the 'Create names dialog box'.
(a) True (b) False

55. An operating system doesn't necessarily manage all devices connected to a system.
(a) True (b) False

56. DNS is a distributed database offering strong consistency and atomicity guarantees.
(a) True (b) False

57. A Hard disk can have move than two heads.
(a) True (b) False

58. AePS stands for Aadhar enabled Payment System.
(a) True (b) False

59. The table and border toolbar is displayed by default when you insert or click a table.
(a) True (b) False

60. A cookie can execute code on your computer.
(a) True (b) False

61. MKDIR is an internal command of DOS.
(a) True (b) False

62. File size is not an important factor when considering inserting an image.
(a) True (b) False

63. Is Search Engine a machine?
(a) True (b) False

64. In power point presentation for animation we select slide and click insert -> animation.
(a) True (b) False

65. To switch back to receiving individual messages send the message set list digests.
(a) True (b) False

66. As you scroll in a document, the insertion point also moves.
(a) True (b) False

67. Count if( ) formula is used in excel for count the number cells with in a range that meet a given condition.
(a) True (b) False

68. On deletion a file removed permanently from disk.
(a) True (b) False

69. Token ring is a computer architecture designed and provided by Microsoft.
(a) True (b) False

70. Group of eight bytes makes an octet.
(a) True (b) False

71. You can't change the font size of title in a PowerPoint slide.

(a) True (b) False

72. RTGS stands for Real Time Gross Settlement.
(a) True (b) False

73. To improve efficiency, servers normally store requested files in a cache memory.
(a) True (b) False

74. Excel cannot insert multiple rows in its sheet.
(a) True (b) False

75. 85 Bingo is a valid name for a cell or a range.
(a) True (b) False

76. Video conferencing is one of the applications of computer where a man is speaking with a man over phone and watching him on screen.
(a) True (b) False

77. CPU is the brain of any computer system.
(a) True (b) False

78. Slide shorter view is the best view to use when setting translation effect for all slides in a presentation.
(a) True (b) False

79. USSD means Unstructured Supplementary Service Data allow users without a smartphone or internet connection to use mobile banking through the *99#.
(a) True (b) False

80. With a single bit you can represent any two distinct items.
(a) True (b) False

81. You can print a PowerPoint presentation in Landscape mode only.
(a) True (b) False

82. CGI is an accepted standard for interfacing web servers and external applications.
(a) True (b) False

83. [Ctrl+H] is used to get help on topics related to power point.
(a) True (b) False

84. Master Card and Visa Card are the types of Credit Cards.
(a) True (b) False

85. New groups are also known as usenet.
(a) True (b) False

86. The amount of money to be charged for a certain amount of insurance coverage is called premium
(a) True (b) False

87. Mail User Agent is a computer program that is used to manage E-mail.
(a) True (b) False

88. By using wizard, we can get ready made presentation file.
(a) True (b) False

89. Rules for exchanging data between computers are called protocols.
(a) True (b) False

90. RTF stands for Rich Text Format.
(a) True (b) False

91. Intel is the biggest player in the microprocessor industry?
(a) True (b) False

92. By default the hyperlink color is blue.
(a) True (b) False

93. Firmware is a software that is embedded in hardware device.
(a) True (b) False

94. An aadhar card is a 12-digit number card.
(a) True (b) False

95. Simple Mail Transfer Protocol is protocol which is used to send and receive mails.
(a) True (b) False

96. Data can be arranged in ascending or descending order by using sort command.
(a) True (b) False

97. [Ctrl+F] performs same operation in MS-word and MS-excel.
(a) True (b) False

98. Windows XP is an example of an Open Source Software program.
(a) True (b) False

99. Star, Bus, Ring, Tree and Graph are the example of network topologies.
(a) True (b) False

100. A blank cell has the numeric value of blank.
(a) True (b) False

Answers

1.	(d)	2.	(b)	3.	(d)	4.	(a)
5.	(b)	6.	(d)	7.	(c)	8.	(c)
9.	(b)	10.	(a)	11.	(a)	12.	(b)
13.	(b)	14.	(d)	15.	(d)	16.	(d)
17.	(a)	18.	(c)	19.	(d)	20.	(a)
21.	(b)	22.	(b)	23.	(b)	24.	(c)
25.	(a)	26.	(a)	27.	(a)	28.	(b)
29.	(c)	30.	(d)	31.	(d)	32.	(a)

33.	(d)	34.	(b)	35.	(a)	36.	(d)
37.	(b)	38.	(c)	39.	(a)	40.	(b)
41.	(d)	42.	(a)	43.	(d)	44.	(d)
45.	(a)	46.	(c)	47.	(b)	48.	(b)
49.	(d)	50.	(a)	51.	(a)	52.	(b)
53.	(b)	54.	(a)	55.	(b)	56.	(a)
57.	(a)	58.	(a)	59.	(a)	60.	(b)
61	(a)	62.	(b)	63.	(b)	64.	(b)
65.	(a)	66.	(b)	67.	(a)	68.	(b)
69.	(b)	70.	(b)	71.	(b)	72.	(a)
73.	(a)	74.	(b)	75.	(b)	76.	(a)
77.	(a)	78.	(a)	79.	(a)	80.	(b)
81.	(b)	82.	(a)	83.	(b)	84.	(a)
85.	(a)	86.	(a)	87.	(a)	88.	(a)
89.	(a)	90.	(a)	91.	(a)	92.	(a)
93.	(a)	94.	(a)	95.	(a)	96.	(a)
97.	(a)	98.	(b)	99.	(a)	100.	(b)

Model Test Paper IX

1. **Which one of the following is related to mobile payment service?**
(a) BHM (b) Google-pay
(c) UPI (d) All of these
2. **Which of the following is not a high level language program?**
(a) C++ (b) C
(c) ADA (d) None of these
3. **When you start PowerPoint, and as long as you don't change the view, you will be working in.**
(a) Slide sorter view (b) Normal view
(c) Outline view (d) Slideshow view
4. **An electronic path, that sends signals from one part of computer to another is–**
(a) Model (b) Logic Gate
(c) Serial Port (d) Bus
5. **Following is the example to Toggle case.**
(a) Toggle case (b) TOGGLE CASE
(c) tOGGLE cASE (d) None of the above
6. **Which of the following devices can be used to input printed text?**
(a) OMR (b) OCR
(c) MICR (d) All of these
7. **Which is used to delete the directory that is empty?**
(a) RD (b) Del
(c) MD (d) Erase
8. **When an inbox mail is deleted accidentally it can be recovered/restorted from.**
(a) Sent mail (b) All mail
(c) Trash (d) Spam mail
9. **In which year was the first e-mail was sens?**
(a) 1995 (b) 1988
(c) 1971 (d) 1975
10. **The most widely used web protocol is–**
(a) http:// (b) ISP
(c) HTML (d) URL
11. **Netscape Navigator is an example of:**
(a) E-Mail Program (b) Internet Browser
(c) Both (a) and (b) (d) None of the above
12. **The slide show button in the custom animation task pane starts the slide show from the:**
(a) From selected slide
(b) From first slide
(c) Last time edited slide
(d) Just back slide of the current slide
13. **Which of the following displays the contents of the active cell?**
(a) Active cell (b) Name box
(c) Formula bar (d) Menu bar
14. **Which among the following is responsible for finding and loading operating system into RAM?**
(a) CMOS (b) Bootstrap Loader
(c) BIOS (d) DMOS
15. **A parallel port is most often used by:**
(a) Mouse (b) Printer
(c) Other Storage Device
(d) Monitor
16. **Cells delete options in a table in MSWord can.**
(a) Shift cell above
(b) Shift the cell to the left
(c) Delete entire row and column
(d) All of the above
17. **In Excel, the cell contain display as '######' when–**
(a) Applied formula is wrong
(b) Wide of cell is insufficients for representation data
(c) When divided by zero
(d) Invalid data
18. **In which menu change case command appears?**
(a) Slide show (b) Insert
(c) Edit (d) Format
19. **Software which allows user to view the web pages is called?**
(a) Interpreter (b) Website
(c) Operating System (d) Internet Browser
20. **In addition to email access, an email service may include.**
(a) An online address book
(b) Instant Messaging
(c) An online calender
(d) All of the above
21. **When writing an email, it is generally a good idea for your paragraphs to be............**
(a) Always intended
(b) Easy to read with large font

(c) Large (d) Small

22. S/MIME in Internet Technology stands for:
(a) Secure Multimedia Internet Mail Extension
(b) Secure Multipurpose Internet Mail Extension
(c) Simple Multimedia Internet Mail Extension
(d) Simple Multipurpose Internet Mail Extension

23. What is full form of TIFF?
(a) Tagged Image File Format
(b) The Image File Format
(c) The Image Fax Format
(d) Tagged Image File Front

24. If you want to copy a selection of text, which button do you click?
(a) Copy (b) Move
(c) Cut (d) Duplicate

25. When a terminal connected to a network validates a password, the checking is done by the:
(a) Graphical User Interface OS
(b) Disk Operating System
(c) Network operating system
(d) Terminal Operating System

26. Which of the following protocol is used for e-mail services.
(a) SMTP (b) SMAP
(c) SMIP (d) SMOP

27. Can illiterate person be issued Debit Card?
(a) Yes
(b) No
(c) In case of head in the family only
(d) In case of joint account only

28. To create a new blank presentation you could ......
(a) Click on new command iin file menu
(b) Click on new button
(c) Both (a) and (b)
(d) None of these

29. Platters that can be tear off are:
(a) Fill color (b) Line color
(c) Font color (d) All of the above

30. Which command is used to select the last cell on the worksheet:
(a) Alt+Ctrl+End (b) Shift+End
(c) Ctr+End (d) Alt+End

31. Excel formulas are made up of
(a) Only from arithmetical operators
(b) Arithmetic operators like = + - and other functions
(c) Only from functions
(d) None of the above

32. You can create a new presentation by using all of the following except:
(a) Click on new file
(b) Ctrl+N
(c) Click on office button and select the new file
(d) Click on open file

33. Which of the following creates a push button?
(a) Reset (b) Check box
(c) Radio (d) Input

34. The processing speed of microcomputer is normally expressed in:
(a) Nautical miles (b) fps
(c) kmph (d) Mhz

35. Generally, emails that you receive will appear in your in ....
(a) inbox (b) contracts
(c) task (d) messenger

36. The slide master includes placeholders for:
(a) Related footer text (b) Date and Time
(c) Slide number (d) All of these

37. .... has a limitations that we can only information to it but cannot or modify it.
(a) Floppy disk (b) Tape drive
(c) Hard disk (d) CD-Rom

38. Which of the following choices is not available in the "select a category" drop down menu of the Insert Function dialog box?
(a) Macro (b) Information
(c) Text (d) User defined

39. Which of the following operating system does not implement multitasking truly?
(a) MS-DOS (b) Windows 98
(c) Windows NT (d) Windows XP

40. In the IP address 192.168.1.1 the first byte is 192. It stands for:
(a) Class A (b) Class B
(c) Class C (d) Class D

41. Extension of Excel file is
(a) .XXL (b) .TMT
(c) .xls (d) None of the above

42. Which of the following methods can be used to enter data in a cell?
(a) Click on formula bar
(b) Press F2 key

(c) Press Tab key (d) All of the above

43. The following is not a valid Cell Address

(a) Sheet 1! 1BC10 (b) Sheet! A1 : cl

(c) Sheet 3!DF6780 (d) Sheet2!HH77

44. For calculation in a spreadsheet, you need to use a:

(a) Table (b) Formula

(c) Variable (d) Field

45. What is the shortcut key to open windows explorer?

(a) Windows Key+W (b) Windows Key+E

(c) Ctrl+O (d) Windows Key+O

46. Access time is

(a) Seek time

(b) Seek time + latency time

(c) Seek time - latency

(d) None of the above

47. .... is not an interpreter.

(a) Java (b) CGI

(c) HTTP (d) HTML

48. Cell address AS4 in a formula means it is a

(a) Absolute cell reference

(b) Relative cell reference

(c) Mixed cell reference

(d) All of the above

49. Operating system is used in ....

(a) Smart card (b) ATM card

(c) Microsoft oven (d) Computer system

50. The area on a slide that holds text that will appear in the presentation online is a ....

(a) Placeholder (b) Text box

(c) Title box (d) Bullet point

51. To use a computer you need an operating system

(a) True (b) False

52. Even though the power supply is on the RAM may lose its stored information due to virus.

(a) True (b) False

53. Power Point allows you to differentiate your animation effects.

(a) True (b) False

54. The first time you save a presentation you must name it.

(a) True (b) False

55. Headers and footers are displayed in the normal view of word.

(a) True (b) False

56. Instagram is more based on mobile compare desktop.

(a) True (b) False

57. Styles can be used to generate a table of contents quickly in the word.

(a) True (b) False

58. Painter Button is used to copy the formatting of a cell.

(a) True (b) False

59. The IP address is divided into 5 classes from A to E.

(a) True (b) False

60. You can ask Excel to count column and rows by using the count () function.

(a) True (b) False

61. A Wide Area Network (WAN) contains two or more LANs.

(a) True (b) False

62. All incoming e-mail message are to be stored in the OUTBOX folder.

(a) True (b) False

63. A protocol used for fetching e-mail from a mail box is POP1.

(a) True (b) False

64. The maximum size of a power point file is 1 MB inclusive of video file.

(a) True (b) False

65. Excel has an autofix when can be used to check the worksheet for spelling errors.

(a) True (b) False

66. A protocol used for fetching e-mail from a mailbox is POP3.

(a) True (b) False

67. Sending information from a client PC to a server computer is called uploading.

(a) True (b) False

68. Refresh button returns to home page.

(a) True (b) False

69. TCP stands for Transmission Control Protocol.

(a) True (b) False

70. Lycos is an internet search engine and web portal..

(a) True (b) False

71. A group of magnetic tapes, video or terminals usually under the control of one master is cluster.

(a) True (b) False

72. The name box is at the left end of the formula bar.

(a) True (b) False

73. Processed data is called information.
(a) True (b) False

74. ATM circuits are appropriate circuits for transmission of voice and real-time data.
(a) True (b) False

75. (Ctrl+A) command select the full page.
(a) True (b) False

76. Sum (Sheet 2 : Sheet 3! B5) adds all the values contained in cell B5 on all the worksheets between and including Sheet 2 and Sheet 3.
(a) True (b) False

77. Port number 143 is used for IMAP protocol.
(a) True (b) False

78. GIF stands for Graphics Interchange Format.
(a) True (b) False

79. Cylinder, cone and pyramid are all chart types.
(a) True (b) False

80. Memory locations are numbered sequentially.
(a) True (b) False

81. A plotter is an output device.
(a) True (b) False

82. (Ctrl+S) command will help you to save a document.
(a) True (b) False

83. Firefly is a type of browser.
(a) True (b) False

84. The decimal equivalent of $(1101)_2$ is 13.
(a) True (b) False

85. MS Excel can be used for generating a Ranom Number.
(a) True (b) False

86. BCD stands for Binary Coded Decimal.
(a) True (b) False

87. 16 is the base of hexa decimal numbers.
(a) True (b) False

88. Valves were used in the 1st generation of computer.
(a) True (b) False

89. Memory has two type—Real memory and Virtual memory.
(a) True (b) False

90. The operating system resides in hard disk.
(a) True (b) False

91. Serial port are used to connect a device such as mouse and modem.
(a) True (b) False

92. Ctrl, Alt and Shift are called Modifier keys.
(a) True (b) False

93. Yahoo, Google and Infoseek are anti-virus.
(a) True (b) False

94. If you connect to a number of personal computers, you will be developing a network.
(a) True (b) False

95. Spam is the term used for unsolicited e-mails.
(a) True (b) False

96. To convert the text message in bold, italic etc., fonts. Rich text and Rich format both will be used by the sender.
(a) True (b) False

97. ARP stands for Auxiliary Resolution Port.
(a) True (b) False

98. Each computr connected to the internet is mandate to have a unique IP address.
(a) True (b) False

99. A program that is used to view websites is called a Browsers.
(a) True (b) False

100. Inkjet and Laser Printers are the examples of Dot Matrix printers.
(a) True (b) False

Answers

1.	(d)	2.	(d)	3.	(b)	4.	(c)
5.	(c)	6.	(b)	7.	(a)	8.	(c)
9.	(c)	10.	(a)	11.	(b)	12.	(a)
13.	(c)	14.	(b)	15.	(b)	16.	(d)
17.	(b)	18.	(d)	19.	(d)	20.	(d)
21.	(a)	22.	(b)	23.	(a)	24.	(a)
25.	(c)	26.	(a)	27.	(a)	28.	(c)
29.	(d)	30.	(c)	31.	(b)	32.	(d)
33.	(d)	34.	(d)	35.	(a)	36.	(d)
37.	(d)	38.	(a)	39.	(a)	40.	(a)
41.	(c)	42.	(d)	43.	(a)	44.	(b)
45.	(b)	46.	(b)	47.	(c)	48.	(c)
49.	(d)	50.	(a)	51.	(a)	52.	(a)
53.	(a)	54.	(a)	55.	(b)	56.	(a)
57.	(a)	58.	(a)	59.	(b)	60.	(a)
61	(a)	62.	(b)	63.	(b)	64.	(b)
65.	(a)	66.	(a)	67.	(a)	68.	(b)

69.	(a)	70.	(a)	71.	(a)	72.	(a)	85.	(b)	86.	(a)	87.	(a)	88.	(a)
73.	(a)	74.	(a)	75.	(a)	76.	(a)	89.	(b)	90.	(a)	91.	(a)	92.	(a)
77.	(a)	78.	(a)	79.	(b)	80.	(a)	93.	(b)	94.	(a)	95.	(a)	96.	(a)
81.	(a)	82.	(a)	83.	(b)	84.	(a)	97.	(b)	98.	(a)	99.	(a)	100.	(b)

Model Test Paper X

1. **What type of computer tool allows you to save data, information and programs into a computer?**
   (a) Storage device (b) Output device
   (c) Telecommunication device
   (d) Input device
2. **Unauthorised access is which type of network issue?**
   (a) Performance (b) Reliability
   (c) Security (d) None of these
3. **Which are the benefit(s) of cloud computer.**
   (a) More safe (b) Low cost
   (c) Fast speed (d) All of these
4. **KYC means**
   (a) Know your character
   (b) Know your customer
   (c) Both (A) and (B)
   (d) None of these
5. **Which network medium is a popular choice for outdoors or in historic buildings?**
   (a) Twisted pair (b) Co-axial cable
   (c) Fibre optics (d) Wireless
6. **Start icon on the desktop is placed on .... bar?**
   (a) Task bar (b) Tool bar
   (c) Menu bar (d) Scroll bar
7. **In excel .... allows users to bring together copies of workbooks that other users have worked on independently.**
   (a) Merge (b) Copy
   (c) Compile (d) Paste
8. **What type of software is used for creating letters, papers and other document?**
   (a) Spreadsheet (b) Operating System
   (c) Word Processor (d) Database
9. **If you receive an urgent-mail that look like it's from your bank, it may actually be a ....**
   (a) Phising attempt (b) Firewall
   (c) Signature (d) Reply to all
10. **Telnet is ....**
    (a) Telephone network
    (b) Terminal network
    (c) Territorial network
    (d) Telecommunication network
11. **Which key is used for the checking spelling?**
    (a) F5 (b) F3
    (c) F9 (d) F7
12. **With most e-mail client programs, an attached file can be ....**
    (a) Examine (b) Detach
    (c) Save (d) All of these
13. **The most popular computer operating system in use today is.**
    (a) Unix (b) Linux
    (c) Macintosh (d) Microsoft Windows
14. **To split a merged cell, select the cell and click the .... button.**
    (a) Split (b) Centre
    (c) Merge and Centre (d) Split and Merge
15. **By default word format your text as ....**
    (a) 12 pt. Times New Toman
    (b) 14 pt. Times New Roman
    (c) 11 pt. Times New Roman
    (d) None of these
16. **Selection of text can be:**
    (a) A paragraph (b) Single word or line
    (c) Entire document (d) All of the above
17. **To display contents of the cell in the centre alignment.**
    (a) Press Ctrl+F
    (b) Press centre button in formatting toolbar
    (c) Press Ctrl+E
    (d) Press Ctrl+D
18. **Which of the following is a type of SSL certificate?**
    (a) WildCard (b) Unified
    (c) Extended (d) All of these
19. **Skype is one of the best.**
    (a) Internet telephony (b) Web browser
    (c) Protocol (d) Web server
20. **Shortcut key for slide show from current slide of the presentation.**
    (a) Shift+F5 (b) F5
    (c) Alt+F5 (d) Ctrl+F5
21. **Which of the following are not required in order to send and receive e-mail?**
    (a) E-mail accounts (b) Use of internet
    (c) E-mail program (d) Webpage
22. **What is the result of this formula "=(5+2)" in Excel.**

(a) 14 (b) 10
(c) 7 (d) 9

23. What type of keys 'ctrl' and 'shift' key are:
(a) Modifier (b) Adjustment
(c) @ (d) Function

24. Where does a header appear in a document?
(a) One the button of each page
(b) On the top of each page
(c) On last page only
(d) On each page only

25. An outcome of a computer virus is:
(a) File erased (b) Motherboard crashed
(c) Program corrupted (d) Disk crashed

26. IP stands for.
(a) Internet Priority (b) Internet Protocol
(c) Internet Property (d) Internet Public

27. PowerPoint presentation is a collection of ....
(a) sound Only images
(c) Slides, handouts, headnotes
(d) video

28. BCC means.
(a) Black carbon copy
(b) Beauty carbon copy
(c) Background color copy
(d) Blind carbon copy

29. The amount of money to be charged for a certain amount of insurance coverage is called?
(a) Cash (b) Token money
(c) Insurance Fund (d) Premium

30. Window shortcut Keys for "SAVE" is ....
(a) Ctrl+S (b) Ctrl+Alt
(c) Ctrl+F1 (d) Ctrl+Q

31. Which of the following functions does not affect the case of a character string?
(a) =PROPER (b) =LEN
(c) =LOWER (d) =UPPER

32. To move down a page in a document the mouse performs:
(a) Wiggle (b) Fly
(c) Scroll (d) Jump

33. E-mail address; separate the user name from the domain name of service provider by using the .... symbol.
(a) @ (b) &
(c) * (d) %

34. QR code stands for:
(a) Quick Restore (b) Quick Result
(c) Quick Response (d) Quick Restore

35. The shortcut key combination for inserting a new slide is ....
(a) Ctrl+M (b) Ctrl+S
(c) Alt+M (d) Ctrl+I

36. To print slide handout, select .... from the menu.
(a) File -> Handout (b) View -> Handout
(c) File -> Print (d) View -> Print

37. What type of computer could be found in a digital watch?
(a) Super computer (b) Mainframe computer
(c) Embedded (d) All of these

38. PPF means:
(a) Person having Pension Facilities
(b) Pension Planning Fund
(c) Permanent Practitioner's
(d) Public Providend Fund

39. Operating system manages:
(a) I/O devices (b) Memory
(c) Processor (d) All of the above

40. URL stands for ....
(a) Universal Resource Identifier
(b) Uniform Resource Identifier
(c) User Resource Identifier
(d) None of these

41. TV and internet inferface is supported by .... devices
(a) Switch (b) Modem only
(c) Modem (d) NIC

42. You can open the Replace dialog box, clicking the replace command on the .... menu.
(a) View (b) File
(c) Edit (d) Tools

43. The least significant bit of the binary number, which is equivalent to any odd decimal number, is
(a) 1 (b) 3
(c) 0 (d) 1 or 0

44. Which connectors can be used with fibre optic network cabling?
(a) RJ-45 (b) ST, FDDI
(c) Both (a) and (b) (d) BNC

45. Portrait and Landscape are:
(a) Page orientation (b) Page size
(c) Page layout (d) Text effect

46. Webpage can be developed by using .... language.

(a) WWW (b) HTML
(c) Internet Explorer (d) Web Browser

47. Comments can be added to cells by using ....

(a) Insert -> Comment (b) Edit -> Comment
(c) View -> Comment (d) File -> Comment

48. The ...... keyboard combination can be used to print a presentation file.

(a) Alt+P (b) Ctrl+P
(c) Ctrl+F (d) F1

49. .... is the name of list that stores the URLs of web pages and links visited in past few days?

(a) Page list (b) Link list
(c) History list (d) All of these

50. .... is the brain of computer:

(a) CPU (b) CU
(c) ALU (d) MU

51. To undo an action while writing into a file.

(a) True (b) False

52. To create a superscript (Ctrl+Shift++) shortcuts is used.

(a) True (b) False

53. In MS Excel, VLOOKUP () function find related records.

(a) True (b) False

54. SATA stands for Serieal Advance Technology Attachment.

(a) True (b) False

55. Graphic tablet belongs to output devices.

(a) True (b) False

56. In MS Word, Page setup option is used to setup document margins.

(a) True (b) False

57. An electronic circuit or software that Compresses or Decompresses videos is known as video codec.

(a) True (b) False

58. CU directs flow of data between CPU and other devices.

(a) True (b) False

59. MS Office, the term ODF for Open Document Format.

(a) True (b) False

60. Interpreter directly executes instructions without previously compiling them into a machine language.

(a) True (b) False

61. A domain name server is a computer that attempts to translate a hostname into an IP address.

(a) True (b) False

62. A system can have more than one web browser installed at the same time.

(a) True (b) False

63. The F1 key displays help on whatever you are working in office.

(a) True (b) False

64. Real operating systems are those which support multi-user capabilities.

(a) True (b) False

65. The data that provides information about other data is known as metadata.

(a) True (b) False

66. VLC player is a video conferencing application.

(a) True (b) False

67. Sir Timothy John "Tim" Berners-Lee is the inventor of WWW.

(a) True (b) False

68. When you click an animation scheme option, it get automatically applied to all slides in the presentation.

(a) True (b) False

69. An Internet service provider (ISP) is a company that provides other companies or individuals with access to the Internet.

(a) True (b) False

70. DNS is a distributed database offering strong consistency and automicity guarantees.

(a) True (b) False

71. Tags are used in a markup language to annotate the information stored in a document.

(a) True (b) False

72. Applets are safer than script, because they are not allowed to read or write to any files.

(a) True (b) False

73. Both DSL, and cable connections are broadband connections.

(a) True (b) False

74. The presentation file previously save can be open by pressing Ctrl+O.

(a) True (b) False

75. Most of the spreadsheet and word processing programs have built in subprograms to convert data into graphs or charts

(a) True (b) False

76. **A list of e-mail address that company has gathered through previous customer contracts, Web sign-up or other permission-based methods is called In-house list.**
(a) True (b) False

77. **Some searh engines index are only the part of a Web page, such as titles and headings.**
(a) True (b) False

78. **A Web browser is a software tool that retrieves and displays Web pages.**
(a) True (b) False

79. **The text editor is used to create, modify and store a text file.**
(a) True (b) False

80. **"Viruses" are not computer programs.**
(a) True (b) False

81. **NEFT services has been started in 2005.**
(a) True (b) False

82. **Data in "TO" field of e-mail message window tells the email server where in send the e-mail messages.**
(a) True (b) False

83. **Python is a first generation programming language.**
(a) True (b) False

84. **We cannot disable popups to appear in the browser.**
(a) True (b) False

85. **You can apply sound effects to animation and apply more than one animation effect to an object or text.**
(a) True (b) False

86. **The size of the table object is dependent on the amount of text within the table.**
(a) True (b) False

87. **TCP/IP defines an abstract interface through which hardware is addressed to hide the diversity of equipment that may be used in a networking environment.**
(a) True (b) False

88. **Filter is used to hide the unwanted data from worksheet.**
(a) True (b) False

89. **Through Graphical users interface in computer, user interacts with machine.**
(a) True (b) False

90. **Primary name of file can be of 10 characters.**
(a) True (b) False

91. **Total number of active cell(s) in a worksheet containing 10 rows and columns is 1.**
(a) True (b) False

92. **In computer hardware, IC stands for Integrated Circuit.**
(a) True (b) False

93. **The maximum file size limit for attachment in Gmail is 1 GB.**
(a) True (b) False

94. **FutureSkills Platforms was launched on 19 February 2018.**
(a) True (b) False

95. **2^{-3} kilobytes is equivalent to 128 bytes.**
(a) True (b) False

96. **The shortcut key to Pop-up windows shutdown is (Win+F4).**
(a) True (b) False

97. **Endnote is added at the end of a document to add explanatory information.**
(a) True (b) False

98. **A Firewall acts a barrier betwen your computer or network and the internet.**
(a) True (b) False

99. **(Ctrl+D) is the shortcut key to open "Font" dialog box.**
(a) True (b) False

100. **The value of MOD (14, 15) in MS Excel is 14.**
(a) True (b) False

Answers

1.	(a)	2.	(c)	3.	(d)	4.	(b)
5.	(d)	6.	(a)	7.	(a)	8.	(c)
9.	(c)	10.	(d)	11.	(d)	12.	(d)
13.	(d)	14.	(d)	15.	(a)	16.	(d)
17.	(b)	18.	(d)	19.	(a)	20.	(a)
21.	(a)	22.	(c)	23.	(a)	24.	(b)
25.	(b)	26.	(b)	27.	(d)	28.	(d)
29.	(d)	30.	(a)	31.	(b)	32.	(c)
33.	(a)	34.	(c)	35.	(a)	36.	(c)
37.	(d)	38.	(d)	39.	(a)	40.	(b)
41.	(b)	42.	(c)	43.	(0)	44.	(c)
45.	(a)	46.	(b)	47.	(a)	48.	(c)
49.	(b)	50.	(a)	51.	(a)	52.	(a)
53.	(a)	54.	(a)	55.	(b)	56.	(a)
57.	(a)	58.	(a)	59.	(a)	60.	(a)
61	(a)	62.	(a)	63.	(a)	64.	(a)

65.	(a)	66.	(b)	67.	(a)	68.	(b)
69.	(a)	70.	(a)	71.	(a)	72.	(a)
73.	(a)	74.	(a)	75.	(a)	76.	(a)
77.	(a)	78.	(a)	79.	(a)	80.	(b)

81.	(a)	82.	(a)	83.	(b)	84.	(b)
85.	(a)	86.	(b)	87.	(a)	88.	(a)
89.	(a)	90.	(b)	91.	(a)	92.	(a)
93.	(b)	94.	(a)	95.	(a)	96.	(b)
97.	(a)	98.	(a)	99.	(a)	100.	(a)

Model Test Paper XI

1. वर्ल्ड का पहला सुपर कम्प्यूटर का क्या नाम है?
   (a) CDC 6600 (b) Cray 1
   (c) Summit (d) UNIVAC

2. 1 Bit is:
   (a) 8 byte (b) 10 byte
   (c) 12 byte (d) 14 byte

3. इंटरनेट क्या है?
   (a) नेटवर्क सिस्टम (b) वेबसाइट का ग्रुप
   (c) सॉफ्टवेयर (d) वेबपेज का ग्रुप

4. Calc में Cell की अधिकतम ऊँचाई क्या होती है?
   (a) .045 cm (b) 0.45 each
   (c) 1.25 cm (d) 1.25 inch

5. आधार कार्ड में कितने डिजिट होते हैं?
   (a) 10 (b) 12
   (c) 14 (d) 15

6. कौन सा नेटवर्क बिल्डिंग के कैंपस तक सीमित है?
   (a) WAN (b) PAN
   (c) LAN (d) All

7. Email के फाउंडर कौन हैं?
   (a) Bill Gates (b) Ray Tomlison
   (c) Steve Jobs (d) None of the above

8. NUUP का पूर्ण रूप क्या है?
   (a) National Unifier USSD Platform
   (b) National Unified USSD Platform
   (c) National Universal USSD Plaform
   (d) None of the above

9. Swift क्या है?
   (a) इसका प्रयोग विदेशों में पैसा ट्रांसफर करने के लिए किया जाता है
   (b) Society for Worldwide Interbank Financial Telecommunication Code
   (c) दोनों
   (d) कोई नहीं

10. Duckduckgo क्या है?
    (a) Search Engine (b) Web Browser
    (c) Network (d) Bird Name

11. NEFT के द्वारा ट्रांजेक्शन लिमिट कितनी होती है?
    (a) 20000 (b) 10000
    (c) 50000 (d) इनमे से कोई नहीं

12. स्प्रेडशीट के पहले Cell में पहुँचने के लिए शॉर्टकट Key क्या है?
    (a) Ctrl+Home (b) Shift+Home
    (c) Ctrl+Pageup (d) Home

13. ट्विटर हैंडल Symbol क्या है?
    (a) # (b) $
    (c) Nota (d) @

14. जीमेल से हम अधिकतम कितने MB तक अटैचमेंट भेज सकते हैं?
    (a) 25 (b) 30
    (c) 20 (d) 15

15. किस कार्ड के लिए पहले से भुगतान करना पड़ता है?
    (a) Debit Card (b) Credit Card
    (c) Goldcard (d) All above

16. अगर मारूति MRF से टायर खरीदती है तो किस प्रकार का व्यवसाय है?
    (a) Customer to Customer
    (b) Business to Business
    (c) Customer to Business
    (d) Business to Customer

17. AI का प्रयोग किस पीढ़ी में हुआ?
    (a) पंचम (b) चतुर्थ
    (c) प्रथम (d) इनमें से कोई नहीं

18. भारत में उमंग एप कब से चालू हुआ?
    (a) 27 नवंबर 2015 (b) 23 नवंबर 2017
    (c) 17 जुलाई 2018 (d) 15 अगस्त 2017

19. ई-मेल में सिग्नेचर कहाँ पर होता है?
    (a) Left (b) Center
    (c) Bottom (d) Right

20. भारत में उमंग एप कितनी भाषाओं में उपलब्ध है?
    (a) 13 (b) 14
    (c) 15 (d) 16

21. WiFi की रेंज कितनी होती है?
    (a) 30 मीटर (b) 90 मीटर
    (c) 100 मीटर (d) (a) और (b) दोनों

22. BHIM App की शुरूआत भारत में कब हुई?
    (a) 6 दिसंबर 2017 (b) 5 नवंबर 2016
    (c) 30 दिसंबर 2016 (d) 26 जनवरी 2018

23. निम्नलिखित में से अलग कौन सी है?
(a) सेंट्रल बैंक (b) स्टेट बैंक ऑफ इंडिया
(c) रिजर्व बैंक ऑफ इंडिया (d) यूनियन बैंक

24. निम्नलिखित 3D में D का मतलब क्या है?
(a) Dimension (b) Display
(c) Discover (d) Division

25. Proprietary सॉफ्टवेयर का दूसरा नाम क्या है?
(a) Open Source Software
(b) Closed Source Software
(c) Freeware
(d) Paid Software

26. DARPA क्या है?
(a) Defence Advanced Research Project Agency
(b) अमेरिका की डिफेंस संगठन
(c) इंटरनेट का निर्माण किया
(d) All of the above

27. CD का आविष्कार किसने किया है?
(a) Tim Berners Lee (b) Jems T. Russel
(c) Marc Anthony (d) None of the above

28. TFT का पूर्ण रूप क्या है?
(a) Thick Film Transistor
(b) Thin Film Transistor
(c) Tubular Film Transistor
(d) None of the above

29. BHIM App के द्वारा एक बार में अधिकतम कितने रूपयों का ट्रांजैक्शन किया जा सकता है?
(a) 10000 (b) 12000
(c) 30000 (d) 40000

30. BHIM App के द्वारा 24 घंटों में कितना ट्रांजैक्शन किया जा सकता है?
(a) 10000 (b) 20000
(c) 40000 (d) 50000

31. UPI के द्वारा अधिकतम कितना पैसा ट्रांसफर कर सकते हैं?
(a) 20000 (b) 10000
(c) 100000 (d) 50000

32. PMSBY का पूर्ण रूप क्या है?
(a) Pradhan Mantri Security Bima Yojna
(b) Pradhan Mantri Secure Bima Yojna
(c) Pradhan Mantri Suraksha Bima Yojna
(d) None

33. NEFT/RTGS द्वारा अधिकतम कितना पैसा ट्रांसफर कर सकते हैं?
(a) 50000 (b) 100000
(c) More than 200000 (d) No limit

34. क्रेडिट कार्ड हमें क्या प्रदान करता है?
(a) Cash (b) Cheque
(c) Cheque or Cash Both
(d) None of the above

35. इंटरनेट के फाउंडर कौन हैं?
(a) ARPA (b) Tim Berners Lee
(c) Charles Babbage (d) IBM

36. भारत में इलेक्ट्रॉनिक वॉलेट कब से चालू हुआ?
(a) 2007 (b) 2010
(c) 2015 (d) 2017

37. लिब्रा ऑफिस में वर्ड काउंट ऑप्शन किस मेन्यू में पाया जाता है?
(a) Insert (b) Tools
(c) Edit Menu (d) Format

38. SMTP का पूरा नाम क्या है?
(a) सिंपल मेल ट्रांसफर प्रोटोकॉल
(b) सिंपल मेलिंग ट्रांसिट प्रोटोकॉल
(c) सिंपल मेल ट्रांसफर प्रोटोकॉल
(d) सब मेल ट्रांसफर प्रोटोकॉल

39. IMEI का पूरा नाम क्या है?
(a) इंटरनेशनल मोबाइल इक्विपमेंट आइडेंटिटी
(b) इंटरनेशनल मोबिलिटी इक्विपमेंट आइडेंटिटी
(c) इंटरनेशनल मोबाइल इक्विप आइडेंटिटी
(d) इंटरनेशनल मोबाइल इक्विपमेंट आइडी

40. गूगल एक सर्च इंजन है?
(a) True (b) False

41. आउटबॉक्स और सेंटबॉक्स एक समान होते हैं?
(a) True (b) Fale

42. इंटरनेट का मालिक गूगल है?
(a) True (b) False

43. दो दोस्तों की ई-मेल आईडी समान हो सकती है?
(a) True (b) False

44. WhatsApp पर हम कभी भी कितनी भी बार नबर बदल सकते हैं?
(a) True (b) False

45. लिब्रा ऑफिस में प्रिंट करने की शॉर्टकट कुंजी क्या होती है?
(a) Ctr+P (b) र1
(c) र1 (d) र1

46. क्या ई-मेल एक से अधिक लोगों को भेजा जा सकता है?
(a) True (b) False

47. क्या हम जीमेल यूजर को बदल सकते हैं?
(a) True (b) False

48. ड्राफ्ट और आउटबॉक्स एक ही हैं?
(a) True (b) False

49. OCR का पूरा नाम क्या है?
(a) ऑप्टिकल कैरेक्टर रिकॉग्निशन
(b) ऑप्टिकल कैर रिकॉग्निशन
(c) ऑप्टिकल कैरेक्टर रिकाड
(d) ऑप्टिकल कैरेक्टर रिसिव

50. जीमेल में यूजर नेम और डोमेन को कौन अलग करता है?
(a) @ (b) #
(c) : (d) ?

51. Paste special shortcut key in Calc?
(a) Ctrl+Shift+V (b) Ctrl+C
(c) Ctrl+Z (d) Ctrl+A

52. Shortcut key to open a document?
(a) Ctrl+0 (b) Ctrl+A
(c) Ctrl+B (d) Ctrl+C

53. NEFT Maximum Amount Deposit?
(a) रा (b) रा
(c) रा (d) No limit

54. Maximum font size in Drop-Down list, Writer?
(a) 6 to 96 (b) 10
(c) 12 (d) 11

55. Ciphers of today is called?
(a) Round Ciphers (b) Cipherstent
(c) Encryption (d) Decryption

56. PIN stands for?
(a) Personal Identification Number
(b) Private Identification Number
(c) Personal Identify Number
(d) Person Identification Number

57. Round(17576,-5)??
(a) 5 (b) Zero
(c) 175 (d) 1756

58. How many digit in Maestro card?
(a) 18 (b) 17
(c) 19 (d) 16

59. माइस्ट्रो कार्ड किस बैंक ने जारी किया?
(a) ICICI (b) Maestro Card
(c) SBI (d) HDFC

60. NEFT सेवा कब तक रहती हैं?
(a) 8.00 am to 7.00 pm (b) 7.00 am to 7.00 pm
(c) 7.00 am to 8.00 pm (d) 8.00 am to 7.00 pm

61. OLX किसके माध्यम से होता है?
(a) B2B (b) B2C
(c) B2C (d) C2B

62. आउटलुक एक्सप्रेस क्या है?
(a) web browser (b) e-mail
(c) web werver (d) web size

63. IMEI नंबर देखने के लिए किस कोड का प्रयोग किया जाता है?
(a) *#06# (b) #07#
(c) #1# (d) #2#

64. Maximum zoom in Libreoffice calc?
(a) 100% (b) 200%
(c) 400% (d) 500%

65. Push button option is available in toolbar.
(a) Insert (b) Format
(c) Tools (d) Slide show

66. Defaults wid in of calc columns?
(a) 2.35 inch (b) 2.5 inch
(c) 2.26 cm (d) 2.5 cm

67. How many photo can upload on facebook at a time?
(a) 25 (b) 30
(c) 35 (d) none of the above

68. Duck Duck is a?
(a) Open System
(b) Web Browser
(c) Application Software
(d) Search Engine

69. Shortcut key of Fill Down?
(a) Ctrl+D (b) Ctrl+A
(c) Ctrl+2 (d) Ctrl+O

70. Auto recovery option is available in writer?
(a) True (b) False

71. Shortcut key clearing all formatting?
(a) Ctrl+A (b) Ctrl+O
(c) Ctrl+M (d) Ctrl+Z

72. Full form of BHIM?
(a) Bharat Interchange for Money
(b) Bharat Interface for Money

(c) Big Interchange for Money
(d) Bhar Interface for Money

73. Full form of EPFO?
(a) Employ Providend Fund
(b) Employee Providend Fund
(c) Employees Providend Fund
(d) E-mail Providend Fund

74. Full form of .png?
(a) Portable Network Graphics
(b) Partable New Graphics
(c) Portable New Graph
(d) Portable Network Graph

75. Maximum limit of UPI?
(a) Rs 100000 (b) Rs 100
(c) Rs 1000 (d) Rs 10,000

76. Full form of DNS?
(a) Domain Now System
(b) Dot Name System
(c) Domain Name System
(d) Domain Network System

77. How many digits in Maestro Card?
(a) 17 to 18 (b) 13 to 19
(c) 16 to 19 (d) 12 to 19

78. Founder of G-mail is:
(a) Paul Buchheit (b) Parul Buchheit
(c) Pal Bachheit (d) Paul Bucheit

79. If NEFT failed then how many working hour or days you money in get refunded
(a) 2 days (b) 1 days
(c) 3 days (d) 4 day

80. To Register in Digilocker you need?
(a) Aadhar Card (b) Pan Card
(c) Your ID Card (d) Passport

81. Found of Facebook?
(a) Paul Buchheit (b) Sunder Pichai
(c) Marc Zuckerberg (d) Bill Gates

82. Can we send message without fill subject?
(a) True (b) False

83. Mozila Firefox is?
(a) Web Site (b) Web Browser
(c) Seb Server (d) Web File

84. USSD was launched by which bank?
(a) NPCI (b) HDFC
(c) SBI (d) UCO

85. एक छिपी हुई स्लाइड एक Slide है जिसे स्लाइड शो चलाने के दौरान दर्शकों को नहीं दिखाया जा सकता?
(a) True (b) False

86. पृष्ठ मार्जिन आपके दस्तावेज के ऊपर, नीचे, बाएं और दाएं, चारों और सफेद स्थान है।
(a) True (b) False

87. Save as रूप का कमांड का उपयोग करते समय आप वास्तव में एक अलग फाइल नाम के साथ अपने मूल दस्तावेज की एक प्रति बनाते हैं?
(a) True (b) False

88. LibreOffice writer के लिए अधिकाधिक फाइल प्रारूप .odt है?
(a) True (b) False

89. LibreOffice Calc में संग्रहित दिनांक और समय को आंतरिक रूप से संख्याओं के रूप में माना जाता है?
(a) True (b) False

90. LibreOffice सॉफ्टवेयर सूट में एक साथ बंडल किए गए कई एप्लीकेशन शामिल होती हैं?
(a) True (b) False

91. LibreOffice केवल खुले दस्तावेज प्रारूप में फाइलों को ओपन और सेव कर सकता है?
(a) True (b) False

92. यदि आप एक मास्टर स्लाइड में एक ग्राफिक जोड़ते हैं तो यह आपकी प्रस्तुति हर स्लाइड पर दिखाई देगा?
(a) True (b) False

93. LibreOffice Impress में एक प्रस्तुति में केवल एक मास्टर स्लाइड हो सकती है?
(a) True (b) False

94. स्प्रेडशीट हमें सारणीवर्धित रूप में डाटा को व्यवस्थित, विश्लेषण और संग्रहित करने की अनुमति देता है?
(a) True (b) False

95. LibreOffice Calc के स्प्रेडशीट में केवल एक शीट हो सकती है?
(a) True (b) False

96. LibreOffice में माइक्रोसॉफ्ट ऑफिस प्रारूप (.docx, .pptx, xlsx) में फाइलों को खोलने और सहेजने के लिए समर्थन शामिल हैं?
(a) True (b) False

97. हम टूलबार को जोड़कर या हटाकर राइटर इंटरफेस को कस्टमाइज कर सकते हैं?
(a) True (b) False

98. LibreOffice Writer में आप माइक्रोसॉफ्ट वर्ड फॉर्मेट में फाइल सेव नहीं कर सकते?

(a) True (b) False

99. LibreOffice Writer में, यदि आप कोई गलती करते हैं (अर्थात् कुछ पाठ को हटा रहे हैं) तो आप इसे अनडू कमांड का उपयोग करके सही कर सकते हैं?

(a) True (b) False

100. आप लिब्रा ऑफिस में एक टेंप्लेट को एडिट नहीं कर सकते?

(a) True (b) False

Answers

1.	(a)	2.	(a)	3.	(a)	4.	(d)
5.	(b)	6.	(c)	7.	(b)	8.	(b)
9.	(c)	10.	(a)	11.	(d)	12.	(a)
13.	(d)	14.	(a)	15.	(a)	16.	(b)
17.	(a)	18.	(b)	19.	(c)	20.	(a)
21.	(d)	22.	(c)	23.	(c)	24.	(a)
25.	(b)	26.	(d)	27.	(b)	28.	(b)
29.	(c)	30.	(c)	31.	(d)	32.	(d)
33.	(d)	34.	(c)	35.	(a)	36.	(b)
37.	(b)	38.	(a)	39.	(a)	40.	(a)
41.	(b)	42.	(b)	43.	(b)	44.	(b)
45.	(a)	46.	(a)	47.	(a)	48.	(b)
49.	(a)	50.	(a)	51.	(a)	52.	(a)
53.	(d)	54.	(a)	55.	(a)	56.	(a)
57.	(b)	58.	(c)	59.	(b)	60.	(a)
61	(c)	62.	(b)	63.	(a)	64.	(c)
65.	(a)	66.	(c)	67.	(b)	68.	(d)
69.	(a)	70.	(a)	71.	(c)	72.	(b)
73.	(c)	74.	(a)	75.	(a)	76.	(c)
77.	(b)	78.	(a)	79.	(b)	80.	(a)
81.	(c)	82.	(a)	83.	(b)	84.	(a)
85.	(a)	86.	(a)	87.	(a)	88.	(a)
89.	(a)	90.	(a)	91.	(b)	92.	(a)
93.	(b)	94.	(a)	95.	(b)	96.	(a)
97.	(a)	98.	(b)	99.	(a)	100.	(b)

Model Test Paper XII

1. **Bit stands for:**
   (a) Binary Digit (b) Binary Information
   (c) Bibariate (d) Bineary Tree

2. **CRT stands for.......**
   (a) Cathode Ray Tub (b) Cathodic Ray Tub
   (c) Cathodic Ray Tube (d) Cathode Ray Tube

3. **The internet is a ....**
   (a) Private Network
   (b) Organization Network
   (c) IS Network (d) Public Network

4. **Internet explorer is a type of?**
   (a) Compiler (b) Operating System
   (c) Browser (d) IP Address

5. **Key used to print a document in LibreOffice writer, Calc and Impress.**
   (a) Ctrl+T (b) Ctrl+F1
   (c) Ctrl+O (d) Ctrl+P

6. **Compiler is used to convert the following to object code which can be executed.**
   (a) Low Level Language
   (b) High Level Language
   (c) Natural Language
   (d) Assembly Language

7. **Which of the following is not including in digital payment system?**
   (a) Mobile Wallet (b) Net Banking
   (c) Cheque Payment (d) None of these

8. **The hexadecimaml number system consists of the following symbols ....**
   (a) 0 – 9 (b) 0 – 7
   (c) 0 – 9, A – F (d) None of these

9. **Data is merged at transport layer before actual delivery at the receiver side this process is known as .....**
   (a) Segmentation (b) Blocking
   (c) Reassembly (d) Packing

10. **One MB is equal to?**
    (a) 1024 Bype (b) 500 GB
    (c) 1024 KB (d) 1000 KB

11. **How much loan amount has been sanctioned by the World Bank (WB) from Gram Panchayats (GPs) development in West Bengal?**
    (a) $210 million (b) $222 million
    (c) $400 million (d) $321 million

12. **To display contents of the cell in the center alignment**
    (a) Press Ctrl+F
    (b) Press Centre Button in Formatting Toolbar
    (c) Ctrl+C (d) Ctrl+D

13. **Data or Information used to run the computer is called ....**
    (a) Hardware (b) Software
    (c) CPU (d) Parriferal

14. **In which of the following LAN configurations do all nodes share a single communication line that carries messages in both directions?**
    (a) Ring Topology (b) Bus Topology
    (c) Start Topology (d) None of these

15. **The most common pointing input devices is**
    (a) Touch Pad (b) Track Ball
    (c) Mouse (d) Touch Screen

16. **The two kinds of main memory are:**
    (a) Random and Sequential
    (b) Primary and Secondary
    (c) Rom and Ram
    (d) All of above

17. **The first electronic computer in the world was?**
    (a) ADVAC (b) UNIVAC
    (c) ENIAC (d) All of above

18. **IIoT stand for ......**
    (a) Intranet of Things
    (b) Industrial Internet of Things
    (c) Internet of Things
    (d) All of above

19. **Which social media is more based on mobile compare desktop.**
    (a) Twitter (b) Facebook
    (c) Instagram (d) None of the above

20. **Hard disk is coated in both side above**
    (a) Optical Metallc Oxide
    (b) Magnetic Metalic Oxide
    (c) Carbon Layer
    (d) All of above

21. **The file type .... indicates the file in a World document.**

(a) .wor (b) .doc
(c) .msw (d) .wrd

22. The Twisted-pair network cable uses which RJ connector?
(a) RJ-14 (b) RJ-15
(c) RJ-45 (d) RJ-25

23. ODF means.........
(a) Open Document Format
(b) Open Door Format
(c) Open Dupp Format
(d) All of above

24. To merge more than one selected cell and click the .... button in Excel.
(a) Split (b) Center
(c) Merge and Center (d) Split and Merge

25. Which command is used to copy files?
(a) Excopy (b) Copy Command
(c) Ctrl+C (d) All of above

26. Which is command is used to change the file name?
(a) Rename (b) Ran
(c) Both (a) and (b) (d) None of these

27. The shortcut key combination for Inserting superscript in LibreOffice Impress is:
(a) Shift+Ctrl+P (b) Shift+Ctrl+B
(c) Alt+M (d) Ctrl+I

28. Which type of software is distributed free but requires the users to pay some amount for further use?
(a) Public Doman Software
(b) Firmware
(c) Abondonware (d) None of these

29. Which one is not found in Window Accessories:
(a) Notpad (b) Wordpad
(c) Paint Brush (d) Internet Explorer

30. To print slide handout, in LibreOffice impress select .... from the menu.
(a) File -> Handout (b) View -> Handout
(c) File -> Print (d) View -> Print

31. Which of the following is word processing software?
(a) MS Word (b) LibreOffice
(c) Easy Word (d) All of above

32. Which of the following keyword shortcuts is used to exit LibreOffice?
(a) Ctrl+Q (b) Ctrl+F4
(c) Ctrl+W (d) Ctrl+E

33. In ASCII, ... characters can be created.
(a) 128 (b) 255
(c) 256 (d) 1024

34. Which of the device does not work in both input and output device?
(a) Light Pen (b) Modem
(c) Mouse (d) CD Rom

35. What is the result of this formula = (22+2)*7 in Excel?
(a) 31 (b) 32
(c) 114 (d) 168

36. NRI means ....
(a) Non Rural Immigrants
(b) Non Rural Individuals
(c) Non Resident Indians
(d) None of the above

37. Which of the following functions does not affect the case of a character string?
(a) =Proper (b) =Len
(c) =Lower (d) =Upper

38. A double sided magnetic disk pack that has six disks normally uses .... surfaces for this pack.
(a) 06 (b) 09
(c) 10 (d) 12

39. Which of the following is not an example of hardware?
(a) Printer (b) Scaner
(c) Mouse (d) Interpreter

40. Comments can be added to cells using ....
(a) Insert -> Comment (b) Edit -> Comment
(c) View -> Comment (d) File -> Comment

41. The diameter of fibre optic cable is expressed in which measurement?
(a) Microns (b) Centimeter
(c) Ohm (d) Milimeter

42. Passwords are used to improve the .... of a network.
(a) Security (b) Speed
(c) Performance (d) Both (a) and (b)

43. With most e-mail client programs, an attached file can be ....
(a) Examine (b) De-attach
(c) Save (d) All of above

44. The underline and center button can be found on the .... toolbar.
(a) Outline (b) Drawing
(c) Formatting (d) Standard

45. You can open the Replace dialog box, by clicking the replace command on the menu.

(a) View (b) File
(c) Edit (d) Tools

46. **A computer's clock speed is measured in:**
(a) Bits (b) Gigabyte
(c) Gigahertz (d) Megabits

47. **The .... keyboard combination can be used to print a presentation file.**
(a) Alt+P (b) Ctrl+F
(c) Ctrl+P (d) F1

48. **........... is the name of list that stores the URLs of web pages and links visited in past few days?**
(a) Page List (b) Link List
(c) History List (d) All of above

49. **If you receive an urgent email that looks like it's from your bank, it may actually be a ....**
(a) C (b) C
(c) S (d) U

50. **Netscape Navigator is an**
(a) E-mail program (b) Internet browser
(c) Both (a) and (b) (d) None of these

51. **You can print a Impress presentation in Landscape mode only.**
(a) True (b) False

52. **A website is a collection of related Web pages.**
(a) True (b) False

53. **An image can be a link to another Web page in an HTML document.**
(a) True (b) False

54. **Ctrl+H is used to get help on topics related to PowerPoint.**
(a) True (b) False

55. **An attribute is an HTML tag that links to another Web page.**
(a) True (b) False

56. **An Extensible Style Sheet Language (XSL) document can be used to transform an XML document.**
(a) True (b) False

57. **If a memory chip can store 100 KB, it can hold approximately 100,000 bytes.**
(a) True (b) False

58. **A LAN becomes a WAN when you expand the network configuration beyond your own premises and must lease data communication lines from a public carrier.**
(a) True (b) False

59. **Bounced emails always result in messages being sent back to the sender.**
(a) True (b) False

60. **One can rename a Impress presentation file when the file is open.**
(a) True (b) False

61. **TCP/IP model uses flow control and congestion management to avoid collision.**
(a) True (b) False

62. **Only one standard design can be maintained in Slide master.**
(a) True (b) False

63. **Network communications were possible before the development of the Web.**
(a) True (b) False

64. **Object on a LibreOffice impress slide that hold text are called Placeholders.**
(a) True (b) False

65. **Any computer on the internet can connect to any other computer on the internet.**
(a) True (b) False

66. **IRDS full form is Remote Desktop Services.**
(a) True (b) False

67. **A browser will usually number an ordered list and used bullets for unordered lists.**
(a) True (b) False

68. **A website might use a cookie to determine the number of unique visitor the site has had.**
(a) True (b) False

69. **FSK is a technique that can be considered as a frequency modulated binary PCM.**
(a) True (b) False

70. **Repeater is circuits' board or card that is installed in a computer so that it can be connected to a network.**
(a) True (b) False

71. **ALU contains CPU, memory boards, device boards, power plugs, etc.**
(a) True (b) False

72. **Icon is not symbolic link to actual program/file.**
(a) True (b) False

73. **HTML documents can be created by using a regular text editor.**
(a) True (b) False

74. **Simple Mail Transfer Protocol is a protocol which is used to send and receive emails.**
(a) True (b) False

75. **A hostname uniquely identifies a particular computer among all others on the Internet.**

(a) True (b) False

76. **Cookie is a message given to a web browser by a web server.**
(a) True (b) False

77. **Every computer connected to an intranet or extranet must have a distinct proxy server.**
(a) True (b) False

78. **CGI is an accepted standard for interfacing web servers and external applications.**
(a) True (b) False

79. **Character size in MS-PowerPoint is measured in font size.**
(a) True (b) False

80. **JPG is an extension of an audio file.**
(a) True (b) False

81. **Most of the spreadsheet and word processing programs have built in subprograms to convert data into graphs or charts.**
(a) True (b) False

82. **A system can have more than one web browser installed at the same time.**
(a) True (b) False

83. **A list of email address that a company has gathered through previous customer contacts, Web sign-ups or other permission-based methods is called In-house list.**
(a) True (b) False

84. **In Impress Presentation for animation we select slide and click Format menu > animation.**
(a) True (b) False

85. **Broadband connections often provide more rapid downloads than uploads.**
(a) True (b) False

86. **The favourite feature on any browser allow saving the URLs of web pages.**
(a) True (b) False

87. **NTFS is a type of Window File Storage.**
(a) True (b) False

88. **Font size can't be changed in Microsoft Word.**
(a) True (b) False

89. **An OS does not necessarily manage all devices connected to a system.**
(a) True (b) False

90. **The presentation file previously save, can be open by pressing Ctrl+O**
(a) True (b) False

91. **HTML includes six predefined heading elements for creating titles and subtitles in documents.**
(a) True (b) False

92. **Umang App can be used in 13 language.**
(a) True (b) False

93. **To name a constant, you use the Create names dialog box.**
(a) True (b) False

94. **Instant message are encrypted before they are sent.**
(a) True (b) False

95. **By dialing *99#, you can take benefits of USSD service.**
(a) True (b) False

96. **Data can be arranged in ascending or descending order by using Sort command.**
(a) True (b) False

97. **A repeater is a network device that duplicate a packate and send the duplicate by an alternate route.**
(a) True (b) False

98. **Transpose function displays row data in a column or column data in a row.**
(a) True (b) False

99. **The Internet is a metropolitan-area network (MAN).**
(a) True (b) False

100. **Message sent over a shared communication line are divided into fixed-size, numbered pieces called packets.**
(a) True (b) False

Answers

1.	(a)	2.	(d)	3.	(d)	4.	(c)
5.	(a)	6.	(b)	7.	(c)	8.	(c)
9.	(d)	10.	(a)	11.	(a)	12.	(b)
13.	(b)	14.	(b)	15.	(c)	16.	(c)
17.	(c)	18.	(b)	19.	(c)	20.	(b)
21.	(b)	22.	(c)	23.	(a)	24.	(c)
25.	(d)	26.	(c)	27.	(a)	28.	(d)
29.	(d)	30.	(c)	31.	(d)	32.	(a)
33.	(a)	34.	(c)	35.	(d)	36.	(c)
37.	(b)	38.	(c)	39.	(d)	40.	(a)
41.	(a)	42.	(a)	43.	(d)	44.	(b)
45.	(c)	46.	(c)	47.	(c)	48.	(c)
49.	(a)	50.	(b)	51.	(b)	52.	(a)
53.	(a)	54.	(b)	55.	(b)	56.	(a)
57.	(b)	58.	(a)	59.	(a)	60.	(b)

61	(a)	62.	(b)	63.	(b)	64.	(a)
65.	(a)	66.	(a)	67.	(a)	68.	(a)
69.	(a)	70.	(b)	71.	(b)	72.	(b)
73.	(a)	74.	(a)	75.	(a)	76.	(a)
77.	(a)	78.	(a)	79.	(a)	80.	(b)

81.	(a)	82.	(a)	83.	(a)	84.	(b)
85.	(a)	86.	(a)	87.	(a)	88.	(b)
89.	(b)	90.	(a)	91.	(a)	92.	(a)
93.	(a)	94.	(b)	95.	(a)	96.	(a)
97.	(b)	98.	(a)	99.	(b)	100.	(a)

Model Test Paper XIII

1. "=MOD(-3,2) entered in a cell displays"
   (a) 1 (b) -1
   (c) 0 (d) -1.5
2. The Simultaneous processing of two or more programs by multiple processors is:
   (a) Multi Processing (b) Multi Tasking
   (c) Multi Programming (d) None of these
3. The line spacing command in LibreOffice can be accessed on the .... menu.
   (a) Edit (b) Format
   (c) Tool (d) View
4. Aadhar card is issued by
   (a) Income Tax Department
   (b) UIDAI
   (c) Nagar Nigam (d) Bank
5. Part number, part description and number of parts ordered are examples of ......
   (a) Feedback (b) Control
   (c) Output (d) Input
6. Who is Bank Mitra?
   (a) Bank employee for help of customer
   (b) Bank customer
   (c) Security of Bank (d) Bank Accountant
7. What do you see at the bottom of Writer & Calc window?
   (a) Task Bar (b) Title Bar
   (c) Menu Bar (d) Status Bar
8. In which of the following LAN configurations is there a center node to which all others are connected?
   (a) Ring Topology (b) Bus Topology
   (c) Star Topology (d) None of these
9. IoT stand for....
   (a) Industry of Things
   (b) Intranet of Things
   (c) Internet of Things
   (d) None of above
10. A client program used to access the Internet services and resources available through the World Wide Web.
    (a) Web Browser (b) ISP
    (c) Web Server (d) None of these
11. Eight bits of data refers to ....
    (a) Riban (b) Clue
    (c) One Bite (d) Ctrl+B
12. The slide show button in the custom animation task pane starts the slide show from the ....
    (a) Selected Slide (b) First Slide
    (c) Last time Edit Slide (d) Back of Present Slide
13. A disk's content that is recorded at the time of manufacture and that cannot be changed or erased by the user is?
    (a) Memory Only (b) Right Only
    (c) Run Only (d) Read Only
14. ISDN stands for
    (a) International Subscriber Dialup Network
    (b) Integeral Service Dianomic Network
    (c) Integerated Service Digital Network
    (d) International Service Digital Network
15. Which of the following is a network device that strengthens and propagates a signal along a long communication line?
    (a) Repeater (b) Modem
    (c) Gateway (d) Router
16. IMPS means Immediate Payment Service managed by ....
    (a) RBI (b) NPCI
    (c) Bank (d) None of above
17. Who can open account under PMJDY?
    (a) Only Ladies (b) Above of age 10 year
    (c) Head of the Family (d) All of above
18. "=ROUND(2.15,1) entered in a cell displays"
    (a) 2.1 (b) 2
    (c) 2.2 (d) None of these
19. The default page orientation in LibreOffice Calc is ....
    (a) Horizontal (b) Landscape
    (c) Portrait (d) None of these
20. HTTP uses .... standard port address
    (a) 80 (b) 75
    (c) 91 (d) 50
21. A .... is an additional set of commands that the computer displays after you make a selection from the main menu.
    (a) Sub Menu (b) Dialog Box
    (c) Menu Selection (d) All of above

22. Select recipients in Mail Merge in Writer consists of following three options ....

(a) Type new list, Use existing list, Select from outlook contact

(b) Type new list, Use existing list, Select from access

(c) Type new list, Use existing list, Select from data source

(d) None of the above

23. .... can store maximum amount of data

(a) Floppy Disk (b) Hard Disk

(c) Compact Disk (d) Magneto Optic Disk

24. Who control credit in India?

(a) Reserve Bank of India

(b) Government of India

(c) Indian Bank

(d) State Bank of India

25. E-mail addresses; separate the user name from the domain name of service provider by using the .... symbol.

(a) @ (b) &

(c) * (d) %

26. .... Number system is usually followed in a typical 32-bit computer.

(a) Hexa Decimal (b) Decimal

(c) Asthadhari (d) Binary

27. A drawer in the bill of exchange can also be a ....

(a) Creditor (b) Banker

(c) Payee (d) Paymaster

28. To create a new blank presentation you could.....

(a) Click on New Command in File Menu

(b) Click on New Button

(c) Both (a) and (b)

(d) None of these

29. Which of the following statements in regard to directories is false?

(a) Directory for delete with file

(b) T Director on High level

(c) Delete a Directory

(d) Not rename a Directory

30. The World Day Against Cyber Censorship (WDACC) is observed on which date?

(a) March 13 (b) March 11

(c) March 10 (d) March 12

31. POS stands for ....

(a) Permanent Server (b) Point of Service

(c) Point of Sale (d) Point of Server

32. As compared to the secondary memory, the primary memory of a computer is..

(a) Cheep (b) Big

(c) Slow (d) Fast

33. The secondary storage devices can only store data but they cannot perform........

(a) Logic Operation

(b) Arithmetic Operation

(c) Fetch Operation

(d) None of the above

34. In Calc charts are created for using which option?

(a) Pi chart (b) Wizard chart

(c) Bar chart (d) None of these

35. The personal computer industry was started by

(a) Apple (b) IBM

(c) HCL (d) Compaq

36. You can open Impress presentation by using all of the following except.

(a) Click on Open Toolbar

(b) Ctrl+O

(c) Click on Open (d) File>New

37. What type of device is a 3.5 inch floppy drive?

(a) Input (b) Output

(c) Storage (d) Software

38. Which of the following is a network device that directs a packet toward its final destination?

(a) Gateway (b) Modem

(c) Node (d) Router

39. Which of the following is a part of the Central Processing Unit.

(a) Printer (b) Keyboard

(c) Arithmetic Logic Unit

(d) Tape

40. The area on a slide that holds text that will appear in the presentation outline is a ....

(a) Texts Box (b) Placeholder

(c) Tital Box (d) Bullet Point

41. Which of the following memories has the shortest access times?

(a) Magnetic Bubble Memory

(b) Cash Memory

(c) RAM

(d) Magnetic Core Memory

42. Calc for the .... function, a formula with a logical function shows the word "TRUE" of "FALSE" as a result ....

(a) And (b) Note
(c) Are (d) If

43. Which of the following edition is available for windows XP?
(a) Professional (b) Business
(c) Extended (d) Developer

44. How are the data organized in a Calc spreadsheet?
(a) Height and Width (b) Line and Space
(c) Row and Column (d) Layer and Plane

45. A DVD is an example of a ......
(a) Output Device
(b) Hard Disk
(c) Solid State Storage Device
(d) Optical Device

46. Computers used the .... number system to store data and perform calculations.
(a) Octal (b) Binary
(c) Hexadecimal (d) Decimal

47. Which of the printer is used to conjunction with computers uses dry ink powder?
(a) Line Printer (b) Daisy Wheel Printer
(c) Laser Printer (d) Dot-Matrix Printer

48. .... is required when more than one person uses a central computer at the same time.
(a) Mouse (b) Terminal
(c) Digitizer (d) Light Pen

49. Which of the following memories allows simultaneous read and writes operations?
(a) RAM (b) ROM
(c) EP ROM (d) None of these

50. "What would you use for immediate, real-time communication with a friend?
(a) E-mail (b) Instant Messageing
(c) Bloge (d) Usenet

51. Credit/Debit Card is a type of plastic card issued by bank or any financial institution.
(a) True (b) False

52. Ctrl+F in outlook express is the shortcut key used to forward a message.
(a) True (b) False

53. Paytm are mobile wallet.
(a) True (b) False

54. CPU is the brain of any computer system.
(a) True (b) False

55. Firmware is software that is embedded in a hardware device.
(a) True (b) False

56. By default the hyperlink color is blue.
(a) True (b) False

57. RTGS stands for Real Time Gross Settlement.
(a) True (b) False

58. Symbolic logic was discovered by George Boole.
(a) True (b) False

59. The Cell/range names are case sensitive.
(a) True (b) False

60. The person who deals with the computer and its management put together are called human ware.
(a) True (b) False

61. If you are going to edit the slide master and the title master, edit the slide master first.
(a) True (b) False

62. Intel is the biggest player in the microprocessor industry.
(a) True (b) False

63. Illiterate person should be issued Debit Card?
(a) True (b) False

64. The Request for Comments (RFCs) core topics are Internet andthe TCP/IP protocol suites.
(a) True (b) False

65. In LibreOffice writer Ctrl+A is used for selecting complete document.
(a) True (b) False

66. An Aadhar card is a 12 digit number card.
(a) True (b) False

67. Modem is a device use for converting an analog signal to a digital signal and back again.
(a) True (b) False

68. LibreOffice impress allow you to differentiate your own animation effects.
(a) True (b) False

69. XML stands for Extensible Markup Language.
(a) True (b) False

70. GIF stands for graphics interchange format.
(a) True (b) False

71. In order to publish a presentation to the web, you must have an active internet connection and the address of the web server that will store your files.
(a) True (b) False

72. To select an entire document in Word, press Ctrl+A.
(a) True (b) False

73. A gray box with a line through it will appear over the slide number that appears below the lower-right corner of a hidden slide.
(a) True (b) False

74. HTML is case sensitive.
(a) True (b) False

75. "A smiley is a sequence of ordinary printable characters, or a small image, intended to represent a human facial expression and convey an emotion."
(a) True (b) False

76. Length () function is used to find the length of the string.
(a) True (b) False

77. Calc can not insert multiple rows in its sheet.
(a) True (b) False

78. Memory locations are numbered sequentially.
(a) True (b) False

79. The full form of ISP is Information Source Provider.
(a) True (b) False

80. Properly arranged data is called information.
(a) True (b) False

81. A(n) Local Area Network connects a relatively small number of machines in a close geographical area.
(a) True (b) False

82. You can apply a color scheme to the current Impress slide or to all slides in your presentation.
(a) True (b) False

83. Task bar is a part of desktop screen.
(a) True (b) False

84. The radix of octal is 7.
(a) True (b) False

85. RMDIR is used to Remove Empty Directory.
(a) True (b) False

86. Linux is an open source operating system.
(a) True (b) False

87. Systems software is a part of software.
(a) True (b) False

88. "Just as you can preview a worksheet before printing, it is not possible to preview a chart."
(a) True (b) False

89. Booting is process of computer start.
(a) True (b) False

90. WordPad is the word processor.
(a) True (b) False

91. Image tags tell the browser how to display images.
(a) True (b) False

92. The Open Systems Interconnection (OSI) reference model is a seven-layer breakdown of network interaction which used to facilitate communication standards.
(a) True (b) False

93. Alt+Space Bar key is used to open control menu in LibreOffice Calc.
(a) True (b) False

94. 99 sales is a valid name for a cell or a range.
(a) True (b) False

95. MKDIR is internal command of DOS.
(a) True (b) False

96. A(n) metropolitan-area network is a large network that covers a college campus, business campus, or city.
(a) True (b) False

97. You can add items to the Start menu of windows.
(a) True (b) False

98. A(n) Wide Area Network connects two or more local-area networks over a potentially large geographic area.
(a) True (b) False

99. The decimal equivalent of $(1101011)_2$ is 107.
(a) True (b) False

100. An illetrate person can also be issued Debit Card.
(a) True (b) False

Answers

1.	(a)	2.	(a)	3.	(b)	4.	(b)
5.	(d)	6.	(a)	7.	(b)	8.	(c)
9.	(c)	10.	(a)	11.	(c)	12.	(a)
13.	(d)	14.	(c)	15.	(a)	16.	(b)
17.	(c)	18.	(c)	19.	(c)	20.	(b)
21.	(a)	22.	(a)	23.	(b)	24.	(a)
25.	(a)	26.	(d)	27.	(c)	28.	(c)
29.	(d)	30.	(d)	31.	(c)	32.	(d)
33.	(d)	34.	(b)	35.	(b)	36.	(d)
37.	(c)	38.	(d)	39.	(c)	40.	(b)
41.	(b)	42.	(d)	43.	(a)	44.	(c)

45.	(d)	46.	(b)	47.	(c)	48.	(b)	73.	(a)	74.	(b)	75.	(a)	76.	(b)
49.	(a)	50.	(b)	51.	(a)	52.	(a)	77.	(a)	78.	(a)	79.	(b)	80.	(a)
53.	(a)	54.	(a)	55.	(a)	56.	(a)	81.	(a)	82.	(a)	83.	(a)	84.	(b)
57.	(a)	58.	(a)	59.	(b)	60.	(a)	85.	(a)	86.	(a)	87.	(a)	88.	(b)
61	(a)	62.	(a)	63.	(a)	64.	(a)	89.	(a)	90.	(a)	91.	(a)	92.	(a)
65.	(a)	66.	(a)	67.	(a)	68.	(a)	93.	(a)	94.	(b)	95.	(a)	96.	(a)
69.	(a)	70.	(a)	71.	(b)	72.	(b)	97.	(a)	98.	(a)	99.	(a)	100.	(a)

Model Test Paper XIV

1. **DNS in internet technology stands for**
   (a) Doman Name System
   (b) Dynamic Name System
   (c) Distributed Name System
   (d) None of the above

2. **Account payee cheques can be paid**
   (a) At ATM
   (b) At cash counter of Bank
   (c) By deposit in Bank Account
   (d) None of the options

3. **Telnet is.....**
   (a) Telephone Network
   (b) Terminal Network
   (c) Terrestrial Network
   (d) Telecommunication Network

4. **To add an additional row to an existing table, you should:**
   (a) Choose Format and then Table
   (b) Choose Table and then Insert and Row above or Row below
   (c) Click on the Tables and Borders button on the Standard Toolbar
   (d) Choose Edit and then Tables

5. **Which is related to virtual reality.**
   (a) Oculus VR (b) Samsung VR
   (c) Google cardboard (d) All of the above

6. **While making nomination, signature of nominee is required on.**
   (a) Account Opening Form
   (b) Affidavit
   (c) Nomination Form
   (d) None of the options

7. **Which of the following is not a valid image format.**
   (a) gif (b) doc
   (c) bmp (d) jpeg

8. **"Accidently, you made a mistake when working with your document. How can you undo that action?"**
   (a) Ctrl+Y (b) Ctrl+X
   (c) Ctrl+U (d) Ctrl+Z

9. **In Writer, the backspace key**
   (a) Deletes the character where the cursor is positioned
   (b) Deletes the character to the left of the cursor
   (c) Deletes a word
   (d) Deletes the character to the right of the cursor

10. **Which is the type of page orientation**
    (a) Landscape (b) Portrait
    (c) Both (a) and (b) (d) Slide

11. **For which of the following task MS Word is not best suited?**
    (a) Creating Slides to show in a workshop or seminar
    (b) Combine main document and data source to send letters too many recipients.
    (c) Writing Thesis
    (d) Automatically formatting pre-written document

12. **Malicious software in known as**
    (a) Maliciousware (b) Badware
    (c) Malware (d) All of the above

13. **Skypee is one of the best**
    (a) Internet Telephony (b) Web Browser
    (c) Protocol (d) Web Server

14. **Which of the following is a common criteria for assenssing web page credibility.**
    (a) Only check to see if the author exists, background information is not important
    (b) Make sure the page is located on a popular web server.
    (c) Only accept sites that have an .edu at the end of their address.
    (d) Check to see if the identity of the page's author is clearly stated.

15. **Computers process data into information by working exclusively with ....**
    (a) Words (b) Characters
    (c) Multimedia (d) Numbers

16. **Which of the following is an output devices?**
    (a) Scanner (b) Plotter
    (c) Light Pen (d) Joystick

17. **OS does not boot itself when a system is ....**
    (a) Reset (b) Shutdown
    (c) Restarted (d) Powered on

18. **Which of the following is used to retrieve or store files on network system?**

(a) DNS (b) FTP
(c) NFS (d) WAIS

19. The following is not a Valid Cell Address.
(a) 1BC10 (b) A190
(c) DF6780 (d) HH77

20. The objective for industry 4.0 is .....
(a) Reduced complexity
(b) Increase efficiency
(c) Enabled self controlling
(d) All above

21. .... is the high speed memory used in the computer.
(a) BIOS (b) RAM
(c) Cache (d) Hard Disk

22. Shortcut key used for paste special in LibreOffice Calc and Impress is:
(a) Shift+F5 (b) F5
(c) Alt+F5 (d) Ctrl+F5

23. Maximum zoom percentage in LibreOffice Impress:
(a) 100 (b) 200
(c) 600 (d) 3000

24. What is the default file extension after .(DOT) in Web files:
(a) .html or .htm (b) .gtml
(c) .xtml (d) .com

25. Computer system consists of
(a) Software (b) Hardware
(c) Both (a) and (b) (d) None of the above

26. Another word for a daisy wheel printer is ....
(a) Petal Printer (b) Line Printer
(c) Laser Printer (d) Golf Ball Printer

27. BCC means:
(a) Black Carbon Copy
(b) Beautiful Carbon Copy
(c) Background Color Copy
(d) Blind Carbon Copy

28. What is the shortcut key to open start menu in Unbuntu?
(a) Ctrl+Esc (b) Press Windows Key
(c) Both (a) and (b) (d) None of these

29. Change case command appears in .... menu.
(a) Insert (b) Tools
(c) Edit (d) Format

30. Printer speed is generally measured in ....
(a) No of character in one page
(b) No of page per second
(c) No of word per second
(d) No of page per minute

31. Formatting of a block of text can be cleared by ....
(a) Selecting AutoFormat
(b) Right clicking mouse
(c) Using key combo Ctrl+F
(d) Using Edit-Clear-Formats

32. The simplest way to break a deadlock is to ....
(a) Lock one of the processes
(b) Rollback
(c) Kill one of the processes
(d) Preempt a resource

33. In LibreOffice Calc the intersection of a row and column is called.
(a) Cubical (b) Square
(c) Worksheet (d) Cell

34. URI stands for ....
(a) Universal Resource Identifier
(b) Uniform Resource Identifier
(c) User Resource Identifier
(d) None of these

35. Which of the following is an example of system software?
(a) Loader (b) Operating System
(c) Linker (d) All of the above

36. IP stands for.
(a) Internet Priority Protocol
(b) Internet Mass Protocol
(c) Internet Property Protocol
(d) Internet Protocol

37. Except for IF and IFERROR, what results from a logical function?
(a) True and False (b) Yes and No
(c) Calculated Value (d) Arithmetic Value

38. An outcome of a computer virus cannot be ....
(a) Deletion of files
(b) Mother Board Crash
(c) Corruption of Program
(d) Disk Crash

39. The internet can be used for
(a) 1 (b) 1
(c) 0 (d) 5

40. The addressing mode(s) that can be used
(a) Accessing complex database
(b) Giving travelling information
(c) Providing notes, lectures and course material
(d) All of the option

41. Nomination once done can ....
(a) Not be cancelled (b) Be cancelled
(c) Not be changed (d) None of the options

42. Key used for subscript the text in LibreOffice writer.
(a) Ctrl+Shift+B (b) Ctrl+Alt+B
(c) Ctrl+O (d) Ctrl+M

43. Maximum font size in LibreOffice writer?
(a) 22 (b) 96
(c) 99 (d) 100

44. Which of the following are not required in order to send and receive e-mail?
(a) 1 (b) 1
(c) 0 (d) 5

45. Impress presentation is a collection of ....
(a) Sound only
(b) Pictures only
(c) Slides, Handouts, Speaker Notes & Outlines
(d) Video only

46. 128.23.120.8 The first byte is 128; This is a class ....
(a) C address (b) A address
(c) B address (d) D address

47. The writer document can be zoomed maximum up to:
(a) 100% (b) 400%
(c) 600% (d) 3000%

48. A .... is a format created by word that uses specific paragraph and character formatting.
(a) Paragraph Style (b) Command
(c) Subparagraph (d) Special Character

49. Can illiterate person be issued Debit Card?
(a) Yes (b) No
(c) Only in case he is head of family
(d) Only in case of joint account

50. Web page can be developed by using .... language.
(a) WWW (b) HTML
(c) Internet Explorer (d) Web Browser

51. As you scroll in a document, the insertion point also moves.
(a) True (b) False

52. E-governance projects involves interactions of the citizen with the govt.
(a) True (b) False

53. It is possible to automatically forward incoming mail to another email address.
(a) True (b) False

54. A web page is mad of two parts: the head and the body.
(a) True (b) False

55. You cannot animate a background image in LibreOffice Impress.
(a) True (b) False

56. In LibreOffice calc spreadsheet, using Ctrl+Shift+; shortcut keys can use to insert time.
(a) True (b) False

57. In LibreOffice Calc, pressing [Ctrl] + [Spacebar] select the entire row
(a) True (b) False

58. An executable file is always a binary file.
(a) True (b) False

59. Mail User Agent (MUA), is a computer program that is used to manage Email.
(a) True (b) False

60. Hybrid clouds combine the public and private clouds.
(a) True (b) False

61. Terminators are used in Bus Topology.
(a) True (b) False

62. Spam does not relates real security and private threats.
(a) True (b) False

63. You cannot undo certain operations like saving, printing, opening and creating documents.
(a) True (b) False

64. Web based e-mail program allow us to check mail from anyone's internet connection.
(a) True (b) False

65. SERP is the abbreviation for Search Enginer Result Pages.
(a) True (b) False

66. The body of the email message is typed directly into the large blank space (message area).
(a) True (b) False

67. Octet is another word for eight byte.
(a) True (b) False

68. **Is Search Engine a machine?**
(a) True (b) False

69. **Token ring is a computer architecture designed and provided by Microsoft.**
(a) True (b) False

70. **You cannot incorporate graphics in a word processor.**
(a) True (b) False

71. **The equipment needed to allow most home computers to connect to the internet is called a peripheral.**
(a) True (b) False

72. **The Restore button appears immediately after a window has been maximized.**
(a) True (b) False

73. **Ctrl+M shortcut is used to insert a new slide in a LibreOffice presentation.**
(a) True (b) False

74. **Small agglomerations of hosts are called sites.**
(a) True (b) False

75. **The FTP means File Transfer Protocol is the client/server program used to retrieve the document.**
(a) True (b) False

76. **Auto correct automatical inserts the text and/or graphics on typing the AutoCorrect entry and pressing the spacebar.**
(a) True (b) False

77. **To connect hub and computer straight through cable is required.**
(a) True (b) False

78. **On deletion a file removed permanently from disk.**
(a) True (b) False

79. **The procedure to create graphics objects is similar to the procedure to draw lines or arrow.**
(a) True (b) False

80. **Compillers are the programmes that translate English like words to high level language.**
(a) True (b) False

81. **Cookies are small pieces of data stored on your computer by the website, so the site can remember you the next time you return to it.**
(a) True (b) False

82. **A blank cell has the numeric value 0.**
(a) True (b) False

83. **Cookies allow a visited website to store its own information about a user on the user's computer.**
(a) True (b) False

84. **Desktop is the screen background and main area of window where icons, taskbar, notification area are appear.**
(a) True (b) False

85. **GUI is used as an interface between hardware and user.**
(a) True (b) False

86. **You can import what you have created in other LibreOffice, such as writer and calc into any of your slides.**
(a) True (b) False

87. **Inbox is the box where incoming mails are stored.**
(a) True (b) False

88. **Becausing of Increasing IM Integration in Popular Application, IM networks are particularly vulnerable to a worm attack.**
(a) True (b) False

89. **One of the option available to the presenter during a slide show is Transitions.**
(a) True (b) False

90. **Key phrase are typed in search bar to get list of sites?**
(a) True (b) False

91. **The solution to availability of DNS is to distribute the information among many computers called DNS Servers.**
(a) True (b) False

92. **UFS stands for Unix File System.**
(a) True (b) False

93. **A mouse comes with exactly three buttons.**
(a) True (b) False

94. **The email message window is used to compose and send an email message.**
(a) True (b) False

95. **Ctrl+F performs same operation in MS-Word and MS-Excel.**
(a) True (b) False

96. **Windows XP is an Example of an Open Source software program.**
(a) True (b) False

97. **To switch back to receiving individual messages, send the message set list digests.**
(a) True (b) False

98. **Optical Mouse uses tiny camera to detect movement.**
(a) True (b) False

99. **Using the undo command (Ctrl+Z) you can undo multiple actions in LibreOffice.**
(a) True (b) False

100. Presentation designs regulate the formating and layour for the slide and are commonly called placeholders.

(a) True (b) False

Answers

1.	(b)	2.	(c)	3.	(c)	4.	(a)
5.	(d)	6.	(d)	7.	(b)	8.	(d)
9.	(b)	10.	(c)	11.	(a)	12.	(d)
13.	(a)	14.	(b)	15.	(d)	16.	(b)
17.	(b)	18.	(b)	19.	(a)	20.	(d)
21.	(c)	22.	(a)	23.	(d)	24.	(a)
25.	(c)	26.	(d)	27.	(d)	28.	(d)
29.	(d)	30.	(d)	31.	(d)	32.	(c)
33.	(d)	34.	(b)	35.	(d)	36.	(d)
37.	(a)	38.	(b)	39.	(c)	40.	(d)
41.	(b)	42.	(a)	43.	(b)	44.	(c)
45.	(c)	46.	(b)	47.	(c)	48.	(a)
49.	(a)	50.	(b)	51.	(b)	52.	(a)
53.	(a)	54.	(a)	55.	(b)	56.	(a)
57.	(b)	58.	(a)	59.	(a)	60.	(a)
61	(a)	62.	(a)	63.	(a)	64.	(a)
65.	(a)	66.	(a)	67.	(b)	68.	(b)
69.	(b)	70.	(b)	71.	(a)	72.	(a)
73.	(a)	74.	(a)	75.	(a)	76.	(a)
77.	(a)	78.	(b)	79.	(a)	80.	(b)
81.	(a)	82.	(a)	83.	(a)	84.	(a)
85.	(a)	86.	(a)	87.	(a)	88.	(a)
89.	(a)	90.	(a)	91.	(a)	92.	(a)
93.	(a)	94.	(a)	95.	(a)	96.	(a)
97.	(a)	98.	(a)	99.	(a)	100.	(a)

Model Test Paper XV

1. **<UL>........</UL> tag is used to ....**
   (a) Underline the text
   (b) Display a bulleted list
   (c) Bold text
   (d) Display a numbered list
2. **A telephone number, a birth date, and a customer name are all examples of ......**
   (a) A database (b) A file
   (c) A record (d) A data
3. **Which is not a type of cloud Computing?**
   (a) Private Cloud (b) Public Cloud
   (c) Hybrid Cloud (d) App Cloud
4. **BIOS is stand for.....**
   (a) Best input output system
   (b) Basic input output system
   (c) Base input output system
   (d) Basic input output symbol
5. **Alignment buttons are available on the .... toolbar in LibreOffice impress.**
   (a) Status Bar (b) Formatting Toolbar
   (c) Standard Toolbar (d) None of the above
6. **Payment through APES is based on .....**
   (a) RBI (b) Aadhar
   (c) Internate (d) Bank
7. **A new printer can be added by:**
   (a) File Manager (b) Control Panel
   (c) View Tools (d) Mozila Group
8. **Another name for an anti-virus is ....**
   (a) Vaccine (b) Spam
   (c) Worm (d) All of above
9. **When an inbox mail is deleted accidentally it can be recovered/restored from**
   (a) Sent Mail (b) All Mail
   (c) Trash (d) Spam Mail
10. **What is default margin in LibreOffice Writer document?**
    (a) 2.1 cm (b) 2.2 cm
    (c) 1.5 cm (d) 2.0 cm
11. **What is the minimum zoom percentage in LibreOffice Impres?**
    (a) 2% (b) 10%
    (c) 5% (d) 30%
12. **.......... is a dead cheque.**
    (a) Stale Cheuqe (b) Post Dated Cheque
    (c) Pre Dated Cheque (d) Antedated Cheque
13. **Which command is used to delete the directory that is empty?**
    (a) RD (b) DEL
    (c) MD (d) Erase
14. **Viruses generally come into the computer from:**
    (a) Surfing (b) CD
    (c) Pen Drive (d) Chaiting
15. **What should be added before a fraction to avoid entering it is a date?**
    (a) // (b) Zero
    (c) FR (d) Zero Space
16. **Inventor of email system?**
    (a) Zuckerberg (b) Allen Turing
    (c) Ray Tomilson (d) Vint Surf
17. **In LibreOffice writer text can be made italic by ....**
    (a) Ctrl+M (b) Ctrl+I
    (c) Ctrl+J (d) Ctrl+L
18. **Minimum font size in LibreOffice writer?**
    (a) 6 (b) 96
    (c) 99 (d) 100
19. **Undo is similar to:.**
    (a) Ctrl+C (b) Ctrl+Z
    (c) Ctrl+X (d) None of these
20. **Which command creates a directory or subdirectory?**
    (a) MKDIR (b) DIR
    (c) MD (d) Both (b) and (c)
21. **First web browser was created in ....**
    (a) 1992 (b) 1991
    (c) 1989 (d) 1990
22. **Unsolicited commercial E-mail is known as ......**
    (a) Spam (b) Mallware
    (c) Virus (d) All of above
23. **The default name of Calc file is ....**
    (a) Workbook 1 (b) Sheet 1
    (c) Book 1 (d) All of above
24. **Linux is a ...... and .... operating system.**
    (a) Multiuser, Multitasking
    (b) Multiuser, Single Tasking

(c) Single User Multitasking
(d) None of the above

25. Models of cloud computing are:
(a) JaaS (b) PaaS
(c) SaaS (d) All of the above

26. What type of computer tool allows you to save data, information, and programs into a computer?
(a) Storage Device
(b) Output Device
(c) Telecommunication Device
(d) Input Device

27. In Excel, When numbers are typed inside a cell, the default alignment is:
(a) Center Aligned (b) Left Aligned
(c) Justified (d) Right Aligned

28. Which network medium is a popular choice for outdoors or in historic buildings?
(a) Twisted Pair (b) Coaxial
(c) Wireless (d) Fibre Optic

29. India's longest cable-stayed bridge across river Narmada is situated on which National Highway (HN)?
(a) NH-5 (b) NH-1
(c) NH-8 (d) NH-2

30. When applying a design to a prresentation, thumbnails of the available design templates are displayed in this section on the pane.
(a) Design Template (b) Outline
(c) Slide (d) Available for Use

31. TV and internet interface are supported by .... device.
(a) Switch (b) Only Modem
(c) Modem (d) NIC

32. Which of the following protocol is used for email services.
(a) SMTP (b) SMAP
(c) SMIP (d) SMOP

33. The least significant bit of the binary number, which is equivalent to any odd decimal number, is
(a) 1 (b) 3
(c) 0 (d) 1 or 0

34. What type of device a computer mouse?
(a) Output (b) Storage
(c) Software (d) Input

35. What type of computer could be found in a digital watch?
(a) Super Computer
(b) Mainframe Computer
(c) Embedded Computer
(d) None of these

36. Which key is used for the checking spelling?
(a) F5 (b) F3
(c) F9 (d) F7

37. What type of keys 'ctrl' and 'shift'?
(a) Modifier (b) Adjustment
(c) @ (d) Function

38. Benefits of Email are?
(a) Cost Effective (b) Fast Speed
(c) Record Keeping (d) All of the above

39. System program threat are ....
(a) Trosen Horse (b) Logic Bomb
(c) Trap Doors (d) All of these

40. .... cloud is accessible on a wide scale:
(a) Public cloud (b) Private cloud
(c) Hybrid cloud (d) Community cloud

41. Which one of the following industrial revolution is known as industry 4.0
(a) First (b) Third
(c) Fourth (d) None of above

42. How many types of cell addressing are available?
(a) 3 (b) 4
(c) 5 (d) 6

43. Devices that enter information and let you to communicate with the computer are called
(a) Input Device
(b) Software
(c) Input/Output Device
(d) Hard Disk

44. ATM password should be kept in?
(a) Office Diary (b) Personal Diary
(c) Memory (d) All of above

45. When writing an email, it is generally a good idea for your paragraphs to be ....
(a) Indented (b) Of large Font
(c) Long (d) Short

46. The instruction for starting a computer are stored in ....
(a) CD-ROM (b) RAM
(c) Processor (d) ROM

47. You can edit existing Excel data by pressing:
(a) F3 Key (b) F1 Key
(c) F2 Key (d) F4 Key

48. **The device on a NIC card that converts the data that it receives from the system into a signal that's appropriate to the network is called ....**
    (a) PROM Chip (b) Port
    (c) Transceiver (d) Receiver
49. **The output devices make it possible to**
    (a) Store Data (b) Look and Print Data
    (c) Data Input (d) None of these
50. **The first Polish antivirus software is**
    (a) Norton (b) mks_vir
    (c) Panda (d) None of above
51. **You may edit word Art by double-clicking it to open the edit word Art dialog box.**
    (a) True (b) False
52. **HTML has a predefined set of tags and XML does not.**
    (a) True (b) False
53. **Without a mouse you cannot work with Windows.**
    (a) True (b) False
54. **RAM memory is not volatile memory**
    (a) True (b) False
55. **An HTML document looks the same in any browser that displays it.**
    (a) True (b) False
56. **An application receiving data is called client Application.**
    (a) True (b) False
57. **Notpaid is a text editor.**
    (a) True (b) False
58. **Unbuntu is an open source operating system.**
    (a) True (b) False
59. **It is considered professional to use nicknames in your e-mail address for work purposes.**
    (a) True (b) False
60. **Character size is measured in point.**
    (a) True (b) False
61. **The text editor is used to create, modify and store a text file.**
    (a) True (b) False
62. **A Web browser is a software tool that retrieves and displays Web pages.**
    (a) True (b) False
63. **A cookie can execute code on your computer.**
    (a) True (b) False
64. **Some search engines index only part of a Web page, such as titles and headings.**
    (a) True (b) False
65. **A browser ignores extra spaces and blank lines in an HTML document.**
    (a) True (b) False
66. **The term NOS stands for Network Operating System.**
    (a) True (b) False
67. **Linux is popular GUI operating system.**
    (a) True (b) False
68. **A link in an HTML document allows an image to be displayed.**
    (a) True (b) False
69. **Whenever you insert a new slide in a LibreOffice impress presentation it is always inserted before the active slide in the slide order.**
    (a) True (b) False
70. **The table and border toolbar is displayed by default when you insert or click a table.**
    (a) True (b) False
71. **From an email address, one can find out the domain name, where this e-mail address is hosted.**
    (a) True (b) False
72. **Some bloggers consider themselves to be "citizen joujrnalists."**
    (a) True (b) False
73. **New groups are also known as usenet.**
    (a) True (b) False
74. **Hard disk can have more than two heads.**
    (a) True (b) False
75. **Extension of MS word document is .docx.**
    (a) True (b) False
76. **Applets are safer than script, because they are not allowed to read or write any files.**
    (a) True (b) False
77. **"Viruses" are not computer programs.**
    (a) True (b) False
78. **You can apply sound effects to animation and apply more than one animation effect to an object or text.**
    (a) True (b) False
79. **Both DSL and cable connections are broadband connections.**
    (a) True (b) False
80. **Tags are used in a markup language to annotate the information stored in a document.**

(a) True (b) False

81. **The custom animation task pane lists the animation effects on a slide in the order in which they were inserted on the slide.**
(a) True (b) False

82. **Several windows can be opened at one time.**
(a) True (b) False

83. **Both save and save as options are used same to save a new file.**
(a) True (b) False

84. **A Web browser is a software tool that retrieves and displays web pages.**
(a) True (b) False

85. **RTF stands for Rich Text Format.**
(a) True (b) False

86. **1 KB is 1024 bytes.**
(a) True (b) False

87. **A file's MIME type indicates the format of files that are attached to email messages.**
(a) True (b) False

88. **A virus is a network security issue.**
(a) True (b) False

89. **Linux is a multi-user, time-sharing system.**
(a) True (b) False

90. **By using Wizard we can get readymade presentation file.**
(a) True (b) False

91. **The Linux file structure is hierarchial.**
(a) True (b) False

92. **It is not possible to rename a folder once made.**
(a) True (b) False

93. **A wide-area network (WAN) connects two or more local-area networks.**
(a) True (b) False

94. **Sir Timothy John "Tim" Berners-Lee is the inventor of www.**
(a) True (b) False

95. **When you click an animation scheme option it is automatically applied to all slides in the presentation.**
(a) True (b) False

96. **An Internet Service Provider (ISP) is a company that provides other companies or individuals with access to the Internet.**
(a) True (b) False

97. **The F1 key displays help on whatever you are working in LibreOffice Writer, Calc and Impress.**
(a) True (b) False

98. **A wide-area network (WAN) connects two or more local-area networks.**
(a) True (b) False

99. **A domain name server is a computer that attempts to translate a hostname into an IP address.**
(a) True (b) False

100. **Linux was introduced by Linux Torvalds in 1991.**
(a) True (b) False

Answers

1.	(d)	2.	(c)	3.	(d)	4.	(b)
5.	(b)	6.	(b)	7.	(b)	8.	(a)
9.	(c)	10.	(c)	11.	(b)	12.	(a)
13.	(a)	14.	(c)	15.	(d)	16.	(c)
17.	(b)	18.	(b)	19.	(b)	20.	(d)
21.	(d)	22.	(a)	23.	(c)	24.	(a)
25.	(a)	26.	(a)	27.	(d)	28.	(c)
29.	(c)	30.	(a)	31.	(b)	32.	(a)
33.	(c)	34.	(d)	35.	(d)	36.	(d)
37.	(a)	38.	(d)	39.	(d)	40.	(a)
41.	(c)	42.	(a)	43.	(a)	44.	(c)
45.	(a)	46.	(d)	47.	(c)	48.	(c)
49.	(b)	50.	(b)	51.	(a)	52.	(a)
53.	(b)	54.	(b)	55.	(b)	56.	(a)
57.	(a)	58.	(a)	59.	(b)	60.	(a)
61	(a)	62.	(a)	63.	(b)	64.	(a)
65.	(a)	66.	(a)	67.	(a)	68.	(b)
69.	(b)	70.	(a)	71.	(a)	72.	(a)
73.	(a)	74.	(a)	75.	(a)	76.	(a)
77.	(b)	78.	(a)	79.	(a)	80.	(a)
81.	(a)	82.	(a)	83.	(a)	84.	(a)
85.	(a)	86.	(a)	87.	(a)	88.	(a)
89.	(a)	90.	(a)	91.	(a)	92.	(b)
93.	(a)	94.	(a)	95.	(b)	96.	(a)
97.	(a)	98.	(a)	99.	(a)	100.	(a)

Model Test Paper XVI

1. **What print command should be selected to print first 5 pages of document?**
   (a) Print preview (b) Page setup
   (c) From .... To .... (d) Print all
2. **The storage capacity of a disk system depends on the bits per inch of track and the tracks per inch of ....**
   (a) Cluster (b) Hum
   (c) Cylinder (d) Surface
3. **............ are the most widely used protocol for LANs.**
   (a) ASP/IP and TCP/IP
   (b) TCP/IP and Ethernet
   (c) Ethernet and Token Ring
   (d) Token Ring and ASP/IP
4. **What is the correct emotion for a regular smiley face?**
   (a) :-) (b) :-(
   (c) :-0 (d) :-p
5. **In LibreOffice Impress you use .... in your slides to hold text, clip art, and charts.**
   (a) Drawing Box (b) Text Box
   (c) Window (d) Placeholders
6. **Number of digit in UPI Pin?**
   (a) 5 (b) 7
   (c) 3-5 (d) 4-6
7. **Which of the following technique develop the Robotics process automation?**
   (a) Artificial Intelliger
   (b) Workflow Automation
   (c) Screen Scraping
   (d) All of the above
8. **In LibreOffice impress maximum handouts in one page is:**
   (a) 6 (b) 9
   (c) 12 (d) 20
9. **Which of the following is not a common type of connector?**
   (a) Parallel Connector (b) USB
   (c) System Bus (d) Serial Connector
10. **To move down a page in a document, the mouse performs ....**
    (a) Wiggle (b) Fly
    (c) Scroll (d) Jump
11. **The most popular computer operating system in use today is.**
    (a) Unix (b) Linux
    (c) Macintosh (d) Microsoft Windows
12. **......... can be reprogrammed by using special external equipment.**
    (a) ROM (b) SAM
    (c) RAM (d) PROM
13. **In LibreOffice Impress, which shortcut key is used to insert a new slide.**
    (a) Ctrl+N (b) Ctrl+M
    (c) Ctrl+D (d) Ctrl+K
14. **The browser's .... keeps a list of web pages you have visited during the current session.**
    (a) Trail (b) Favourites
    (c) History (d) Cache
15. **The search result presented in a line of results are called is:**
    (a) Search engine result pages
    (b) Search engine pages
    (c) Category list (d) Tag lists
16. **Which method cannot be used to enter data in a cell of Excel sheet press .... key?**
    (a) Enter Key (b) Arrow Key
    (c) Tab Key (d) Esc Key
17. **Is a protocol that is defined in several RFC's.**
    (a) Java Script (b) XML
    (c) HTML (d) HTTP
18. **Output of the excel 2013 expression is =10*2.**
    (a) 8 (b) 16
    (c) 20 (d) 32
19. **Mail user agent, is also called:**
    (a) Mail Server (b) Email Client
    (c) Mail User (d) Mail Provider
20. **Typewriter is a type of ....**
    (a) Transition (b) Notes Pages
    (c) Slide (d) Ctrl+B, Brush
21. **The internet was originally developed by ....**
    (a) Computer Hackers
    (b) A Corporation
    (c) The University of Michigan

(d) The U.S. Department of Defense

22. The Wizard of the Impress includes ....

(a) Auto content wizard
(b) Auto content and pick a look wizard
(c) Pick a look wizard
(d) Chart wizard and auto content wizard

23. Mailing list is a way of having a..........

(a) Private discussion
(b) No discussion
(c) Non-public discussion
(d) Public discussion

24. Email address consists of:

(a) Home address
(b) Domain address of Mail server
(c) ISP name
(d) User identification

25. In a synchronous modem, the receive equilizer is known as:

(a) Adaptive equilizer
(b) Compromise equilizer
(c) Statistial equilizer
(d) Impariment equilier

26. The safest place for keeping money

(a) A pit dug in the ground
(b) Money lender
(c) Bank (d) An iron box

27. In Calc spreadsheet, when numbers are typed a cell, the default alignment is:

(a) Center aligned (b) Left aligned
(c) Justified (d) Right aligned

28. Which is not a service of cloud Computing?

(a) Platform as a service
(b) Software as a service
(c) Hardware as a servie
(d) All of the above

29. The most widely used web protocol is.

(a) HTTP:// (b) ISP
(c) HTML (d) URL

30. Window Shortcut keys for "SAVE" is ....

(a) Ctrl+S (b) Ctrl+Alt
(c) Ctrl+F1 (d) Ctrl+Q

31. Capital letters on a keyboard are ....

(a) Upper case letter (b) Grownups
(c) Caps lock key (d) Big Guys

32. If you wish to send a received message on to someone who wasn't in the original recipients' list, use the .... command.

(a) Forward all (b) Forward
(c) Broadcast (d) Reply all

33. Which of the following server acts as a mediator between client and other servers?

(a) Gaming Server
(b) Intermediate Server
(c) Printing Server
(d) Proxy Server

34. Interest on Saving Deposit is paid.

(a) Every Month (b) Yearly
(c) Quarterly (d) Half Yearly

35. Which Protocol is used for file transferring:

(a) FTP (b) HTTP
(c) TCP (d) SMTP

36. The highest data rate is provided by the .... transmission medium.

(a) Optical Fiber (b) Microwave
(c) Coaxial cable (d) Twisted Pair

37. What type of software is used for creating letters papers and other documents?

(a) Spreadsheet (b) Operating System
(c) Word Processor (d) Database

38. A unique string of bits, or the binary pattern, of a virus is known as:

(a) Virun Pattern (b) Virus Bit
(c) Virus Signature (d) All of these

39. Software which allows user to view the webpage is called as:

(a) Interpreter (b) Website
(c) Operating System (d) Internet Browser

40. On the Internet, a flame is a message that is ....

(a) Typed with a lot of mistakes
(b) Typed with different font sizes
(c) Typed in all capital letters
(d) Typed n anger

41. A shortcut key used to operate function in LibreOffice Calc.

(a) Alt+F2 (b) Ctrl+F2
(c) Ctrl+Shift+O (d) Ctrl+F

42. .... is not an interpreter.

(a) Java (b) CGI
(c) HTTP (d) HTML

43. **In LibreOffice Portrait and Landscape are:**
(a) Page Orientation (b) Page size
(c) Page Layout (d) Texts Effects

44. **When sending an e-mail, the line describes the contents of the message.**
(a) To (b) Contents
(c) CC (d) Subject

45. **Which of the following is an example of malware?**
(a) An evil turn (b) A zombie
(c) A virus (d) All of these

46. **A file without extension .... in MS DOS.**
(a) Executable
(b) Is not recognizable
(c) Document file
(d) Represents database file

47. **A function inside another function is called a .... function.**
(a) Text (b) Sum
(c) Round (d) Nested

48. **Operating system manages?**
(a) I/O Devices (b) Memory
(c) Processor (d) All of the options

49. **Mathematical calculation in a spreadsheet are called?**
(a) Labels (b) Words
(c) Formulas (d) Values

50. **Which of the following creates a push button?**
(a) Reset (b) Check Box
(c) Radio (d) Input

51. **Mouse speed is adjustable.**
(a) True (b) False

52. **A Linux OS is portable.**
(a) True (b) False

53. **Console is computer's hard drive, keyboard and screen.**
(a) True (b) False

54. **A method of advancing slides is called Motion Path.**
(a) True (b) False

55. **Line color and style includes special effects that can be applied to drawing object.**
(a) True (b) False

56. **Cache memory is much faster than RAM.**
(a) True (b) False

57. **In private filtering one can prevent the websites from automatically sharing details about your visit with third-party content provider websites.**
(a) True (b) False

58. **The maximum size of a PowerPoint file is 1 MB inclusive of video file.**
(a) True (b) False

59. **Statistical operations are not allowed in Excel 2013.**
(a) True (b) False

60. **In LibreOffice Ctrl+M shortcut key is use to clear direct formating.**
(a) True (b) False

61. **Internet is a network of computers linking many different types of computers all over the world.**
(a) True (b) False

62. **Device Drivers are specialized programs designed to allow particular input and output devices to communicate with the rest of the computer.**
(a) True (b) False

63. **In LibreOffice writer document Ctrl+Alt+C is used to insert comment.**
(a) True (b) False

64. **A printer can be removed from Windows OS by removing its icon from desktop.**
(a) True (b) False

65. **The act of exploring web is known as surfing.**
(a) True (b) False

66. **E-mail spoofing occurs when the header information of an email is altered so that it appear to come from a trusted source**
(a) True (b) False

67. **WAN can span across entire country.**
(a) True (b) False

68. **The ability to compose a message, check your email, and reply to a message is basic email skills.**
(a) True (b) False

69. **HTML stands for Hypertext Mark-up Language.**
(a) True (b) False

70. **Google chrome is the web broswer.**
(a) True (b) False

71. **We can navigate all pages in Print Preview.**
(a) True (b) False

72. **The uniform resource locator (URL) is a standard for specifying any kind of information on the internet.**
(a) True (b) False

73. **It is possible to add new slide using common task buttons.**
(a) True (b) False

74. **UFS stands for Unix File System.**
(a) True (b) False

75. **A web browser is a software program that allows you to browse, search and receive various types of information such as websites.**
(a) True (b) False

76. **When you copy a formula a LibreOffice Calc spreadsheet, relative cell reference do not change.**
(a) True (b) False

77. **Search Engines maintain heavy database of keywords and URL's?**
(a) True (b) False

78. **Operating System manages Monitor and Printer.**
(a) True (b) False

79. **Gpay created by google.**
(a) True (b) False

80. **X.25 is an example of packet switched network.**
(a) True (b) False

81. **Sum() functions offers you the possibility to view different results depending on the entered condition.**
(a) True (b) False

82. **Hackers, Virus and Worms are security and privacy threats.**
(a) True (b) False

83. **IETF stands for Internet Engineering Task Force.**
(a) True (b) False

84. **A blank line is also called as paragraph.**
(a) True (b) False

85. **Margins are the distances between the text and the edges of the paper.**
(a) True (b) False

86. **The area on the task bar that displays time is called notification area.**
(a) True (b) False

87. **Worms can not affect instant messaging applications.**
(a) True (b) False

88. **Italic characters are slanted than regular characters.**
(a) True (b) False

89. **The AutoContent Wizard creates the structure and contents based on the choice you make.**
(a) True (b) False

90. **The sites visited by you are removed from the drop down box address bar by deleting cookies.**
(a) True (b) False

91. **Information is carried in data communication thousands of kilometres.**
(a) True (b) False

92. **In an email client program, messages can be sorted by clicking the column heading once by which you wish to sort A–Z.**
(a) True (b) False

93. **Len() function is used to find the length of the string.**
(a) True (b) False

94. **MTA stands for Mail Transfer Agent.**
(a) True (b) False

95. **A user wants to copy a file to another location; the request line contains the copy method.**
(a) True (b) False

96. **Is it possible to save in your computer downloaded web page(s) from website.**
(a) True (b) False

97. **In <IMG SRC="Pictures/book1.gif" ALIGN=middle> ALIGN is an attribute.**
(a) True (b) False

98. **Rules and norms are part of the unique identity of any social collective.**
(a) True (b) False

99. **In LibreOffice Calc sheet Ctrl+;] shortcut key is used to insert current date in a cell.**
(a) True (b) False

100. **Copying files from your computer to another computer on the Internet is called uploading.**
(a) True (b) False

Answers

1.	(c)	2.	(d)	3.	(c)	4.	(a)
5.	(d)	6.	(d)	7.	(d)	8.	(b)
9.	(c)	10.	(c)	11.	(d)	12.	(d)
13.	(b)	14.	(c)	15.	(a)	16.	(d)
17.	(d)	18.	(c)	19.	(b)	20.	(d)
21.	(d)	22.	(a)	23.	(a)	24.	(b)
25.	(a)	26.	(c)	27.	(d)	28.	(c)
29.	(a)	30.	(a)	31.	(c)	32.	(b)
33.	(d)	34.	(d)	35.	(a)	36.	(a)
37.	(c)	38.	(c)	39.	(d)	40.	(d)
41.	(b)	42.	(c)	43.	(a)	44.	(d)
45.	(c)	46.	(b)	47.	(d)	48.	(d)
49.	(c)	50.	(d)	51.	(a)	52.	(a)

53.	(b)	54.	(b)	55.	(a)	56.	(a)	77.	(a)	78.	(a)	79.	(a)	80.	(a)
57.	(a)	58.	(b)	59.	(b)	60.	(a)	81.	(b)	82.	(a)	83.	(a)	84.	(a)
61	(a)	62.	(a)	63.	(a)	64.	(b)	85.	(a)	86.	(a)	87.	(b)	88.	(a)
65.	(a)	66.	(a)	67.	(a)	68.	(a)	89.	(a)	90.	(a)	91.	(a)	92.	(b)
69.	(a)	70.	(a)	71.	(a)	72.	(a)	93.	(a)	94.	(a)	95.	(a)	96.	(a)
73.	(a)	74.	(a)	75.	(a)	76.	(b)	97.	(a)	98.	(a)	99.	(a)	100.	(a)

Model Test Paper XVII

1. **The formula that will add the value of cell D4 to the value of C2 and then multiple by the value in B2 in Calc is....**
   (a) D4+C2*B2 (b) (D4+C2)*B2
   (c) =(B2*(D4+C2) (d) =(D4+C2)*B2
2. **In latest generation computers, the instructions are executed?**
   (a) Serial Type (b) Parallel Type
   (c) Pipeline Type (d) None of these
3. **Internet of things is..**
   (a) Machine World (b) Computer Network
   (c) Physical World (d) All of the above
4. **3D printer is a type of........**
   (a) Virtual Reality (b) Industrial Robot
   (c) Cryptographic (d) None of the above
5. **Which of the following protocols is used by internet mail?**
   (a) TCP/IP (b) HTTP
   (c) FTP (d) None of these
6. **Small network making up the internet and having a small number of computers within it is called....**
   (a) Address (b) Host
   (c) Sub-station (d) None
7. **How can you stop slide show LibreOffice Impress?**
   (a) Press Esc Key
   (b) Press Left Arrow Key
   (c) Press Down Arrow Key
   (d) None of these
8. **Malwares spread by infecting computers in many ways through ....**
   (a) E-mails (b) Portable Disk
   (c) File Downloads (d) CD-Roms
9. **The following is a slide transition effect in LibreOffice Impress.**
   (a) Fine Desalve (b) Vipe all over
   (c) Bit by Bit (d) None of these
10. **Which of the following view is not one of LibreOffice impress presentation view?**
    (a) Normal View (b) Slide Sorter View
    (c) Both (a) and (b) (d) Sorter View
11. **E-mail address is made up of**
    (a) Two part (b) One part
    (c) Three part (d) None of these
12. **A gigabyte is equal to.**
    (a) 1024 Megabyte
    (b) One Thousand Kilobyte
    (c) 1 Billion Megabyte
    (d) 1024*1024 Megabyte
13. **When a computer prints a report, this output is called:**
    (a) Soft Copy (b) Hard Copy
    (c) COM (d) None of these
14. **With the email we can attach the file**
    (a) Three (b) Four
    (c) One (d) Two
15. **Some web pages are divided into independent panes names as:**
    (a) Windows (b) Tiles
    (c) Frames (d) None of these
16. **Personal computers use a number of chips mounted on a main circuit board. What is the common name for such boards?**
    (a) Motherboard (b) Ethernet
    (c) Green Board (d) Red Board
17. **A function in LibreOffice Calc**
    (a) Calculation for normal and typical
    (b) A Readymade Formula
    (c) Open with a Symbol
    (d) None of these
18. **Internet is:**
    (a) Network of Network
    (b) Prouded by ISP
    (c) Speed over thousands of kilometres
    (d) All of the above
19. **A computer which links several PCs together in a network is called:**
    (a) Server (b) Mini Computer
    (c) Main Frame (d) Client
20. **If a computer is on but does not respond, what is it said to be?**
    (a) Hand (b) Sleepmode
    (c) Hibernate (d) None of these
21. **In writer document selection of text can be of..**
    (a) One Paragraph
    (b) Single word or One line

(c) Complete Document
(d) All of the above

22. Which of the following is not a type of DVD drive?
(a) DVD+RW (b) DVD+RAM
(c) DVD+RW (d) DVD+RD

23. Which of the following is not a high level language program?
(a) C++ (b) C
(c) ADA (d) None of these

24. Which of the following devices can be used to input printed text?
(a) OMR (b) OCR
(c) MICR (d) All of the above

25. The operating system for a computer does:
(a) Managed to computer resources
(b) Managed to disk and file
(c) Managed to computer memory
(d) All of above

26. Optimizes the column width or row height based on the current cell.
(a) Ctrl+F2 (b) Alt+End
(c) Alt+Right Arrow Key
(d) F2

27. .... is the menu command to create a text box on a LibreOffice Presentation slide.
(a) View/Text Box (b) Tool/Text Box
(c) Format/Text Box (d) Insert/Text Box

28. A host on the internet finds another host by its:
(a) By Electronic Address
(b) By Postal Address
(c) By IP Address (d) None of these

29. Moves the cursor to the first cell in the sheet (A1) in LibreOffice.
(a) Ctrl+Home (b) Ctrl+F1
(c) Ctrl+O (d) Alt+F1

30. Which of the following is related to internet security?
(a) CERT (b) W3C
(c) DSL (d) MIT

31. Where does a header appear in a document in LibreOffice?
(a) Bottom on every page
(b) Top on every page
(c) Only first page (d) Only last page

32. The paper orientation for printing is
(a) Landscape (b) Portrait
(c) Both (a) and (b) (d) None of these

33. How many spreadsheet are on LibreOffice calc by default?
(a) 0 (b) 1
(c) 2 (d) 3

34. Number of Rows in LibreOffice Calc spreadsheet?
(a) 21,000,571 (b) 1,048,576
(c) 100000 (d) 1,000,571

35. LibreOffice Writer document text can be made italic:
(a) Ctrl+M (b) Ctrl+1
(c) Al+J (d) Ctrl+L

36. Which command is used for print preview in LibreOffice Writer...
(a) Print>Print Preview
(b) Shift+Ctrl+O
(c) Layout>Print Preview
(d) Ctrl+P

37. Which topology requires a multipoint connection?
(a) Bush (b) Ring
(c) Mash (d) Star

38. .... is the example of block chain Technique.
(a) Bitcoin (b) Processor
(c) Bit and Byte (d) None of the above

39. Address 127.0.0.0 is called the ....
(a) Reserve Address (b) Mac Address
(c) Multicast Address (d) Broadcast Address

40. A parallel port is most often used by....
(a) Mouse (b) Printer
(c) Other Storage Devices
(d) Monitor

41. S/SIME in Internet technology stands for?
(a) Secure/Multimedia Internet Mail Extension
(b) Secure/Multipurpose Internet Mail Extension
(c) Simple/Multimedia Internet Mail Extension
(d) Simple/Multipurpose Internet Mail Extension

42. LAN is:
(a) Locate All Network
(b) Local Area Network
(c) Label Area Network
(d) Local Area None

43. E-wallet is used for:
(a) Cash payment (b) Check payment
(c) Digital payment (d) None of these

44. For calculation in a Calc spreadsheet, you need to use a:

(a) Table (b) Formula
(c) Variable (d) Field

45. **To make a field name in the data sources is not permitted.**
(a) Number (b) Letter
(c) Space (d) Underscore character

46. **......... has a limitation that we can only add information to it but cannot or modify it.**
(a) Floppy Disk (b) Tape Drive
(c) Hard Disk (d) CD Rom

47. **The processing speed of a microcomputer is normally expressed in:**
(a) Nautical Miles (b) Feet/Second
(c) Kilometer/Hours (d) Megahertz

48. **Cell address A$4 in a formula means it is a:**
(a) Absolute Cell Reference
(b) Relative Cell Reference
(c) Mixed Cell Reference
(d) All of the above

49. **When you delete the mails, they are moved to .... folder.**
(a) Outlook (b) Inbox
(c) Trash (d) Recycle bin

50. **LibreOffice Calc formulas are made up of .....**
(a) Only Arithmetic operators
(b) Arithmetic operators as =+- and other function
(c) Only function
(d) None of the above

51. **Splitting a cell results in two cells of equal width.**
(a) True (b) False

52. **Format painter button is used to copy the formatting of a cell.**
(a) True (b) False

53. **LibreOffice calc spreadsheet prints gridlines by default.**
(a) True (b) False

54. **The slide sorter view button automatically sorts the slides alphabetically.**
(a) True (b) False

55. **A hardened firewall host on an internet allows specified internet users to access specified services in the internet.**
(a) True (b) False

56. **You cannot move or copy sheets from one workbook to another.**
(a) True (b) False

57. **In LibreOffice Calc spreadsheet Ctrl+H is used to display find and replace dialog box.**
(a) True (b) False

58. **ALU is a part of CPU.**
(a) True (b) False

59. **In LibreOffice Calc spreadsheet cannot insert multiple rows in its sheet.**
(a) True (b) False

60. **When a formatted number does not fit in a cell, number signs like has (####) are displayed.**
(a) True (b) False

61. **WWW is a large-scale implementation of client-server architecture.**
(a) True (b) False

62. **The two parts of an e-mail address is separated by @ symbol**
(a) True (b) False

63. **Scripting languages cannot be displayed in your browser.**
(a) True (b) False

64. **All the web servers on the Internet are collectively referred to as the World Wide Web.**
(a) True (b) False

65. **QR code available in Phone pe.**
(a) True (b) False

66. **Different elements in a chart cannot have different transition.**
(a) True (b) False

67. **Calc is used only as spreadsheet and offers no graphics, database and word processing features.**
(a) True (b) False

68. **The IP address is divided into classes five, which are given letters A through E.**
(a) True (b) False

69. **In Calc, standard width of a column is 8.43.**
(a) True (b) False

70. **ISP is a company that provides an Internet connection.**
(a) True (b) False

71. **Even through the power supply is on, the RAM may lose its stored information, due to virus.**
(a) True (b) False

72. **The most common type of toner-based printer is the inkjet printer.**
(a) True (b) False

73. VDUs can be used both as an input and output devices.
(a) True (b) False
74. We can access data randomly which is stored on magnetic tape.
(a) True (b) False
75. The act of exploring web is known as surfing.
(a) True (b) False
76. Multi-keyword queries take a longer time to produce results in a search engine than single word queries.
(a) True (b) False
77. The email address only requires user name.
(a) True (b) False
78. In UPI payment system Virtual Payment Address is mandatry.
(a) True (b) False
79. You can add drawing objects and pictures to paid pages.
(a) True (b) False
80. Bold, underline, and Italics are available in the Formatting toolbar.
(a) True (b) False
81. MIME defines mechanisms for sending other kinds of information in e-mail, such as files containing images, sounds, movies, and computer programe.
(a) True (b) False
82. Email that is sent to you is stored on your mail server until you retrieve your messages.
(a) True (b) False
83. If a dialog box has 4 radio buttons in the same group, you may choose any one of them.
(a) True (b) False
84. Aligning text is same as indenting text.
(a) True (b) False
85. A footer is printed at the bottom of every page.
(a) True (b) False
86. Fetching of an instruction for execution is done by the control unit.
(a) True (b) False
87. The programs (instructions) that tell the computer what to do is termed as hardware.
(a) True (b) False
88. Linkedin is a business and professional networking site is launched in 5th May 2003.
(a) True (b) False
89. Microsoft Word first identifies a grammatical error followed by spelling error.
(a) True (b) False
90. Primary memory has higher storage capacity than secondary memory.
(a) True (b) False
91. The (Shift)+(Tab) shortcut key moves the mouse pointer to the next cell LibreOffice writer table.
(a) True (b) False
92. Linux was introduced by Linux Torvalds in 1991.
(a) True (b) False
93. Is decentralization one of the design principles for industry 4.0?
(a) True (b) False
94. UTR means Unique Transaction Reference.
(a) True (b) False
95. Print button on the standard toolbar will print the entire document using the default settings.
(a) True (b) False
96. In LibreOffice using Ctrl+U shortcut key(s) can underline the selected text.
(a) True (b) False
97. You can insert manual page breaks when you want to force a page break.
(a) True (b) False
98. The same header is necessarily printed on all even pages of the document.
(a) True (b) False
99. The current date cannot be inserted in the header.
(a) True (b) False
100. LibreOffice impress template does not include style formatting.
(a) True (b) False

Answers

1.	(d)	2.	(d)	3.	(c)	4.	(b)
5.	(d)	6.	(b)	7.	(a)	8.	(c)
9.	(a)	10.	(d)	11.	(c)	12.	(a)
13.	(b)	14.	(d)	15.	(c)	16.	(a)
17.	(b)	18.	(d)	19.	(a)	20.	(a)
21.	(d)	22.	(d)	23.	(d)	24.	(b)
25.	(d)	26.	(c)	27.	(d)	28.	(c)
29.	(a)	30.	(a)	31.	(b)	32.	(c)
33.	(b)	34.	(b)	35.	(b)	36.	(b)

37.	(a)	38.	(c)	39.	(b)	40.	(b)	69.	(a)	70.	(a)	71.	(a)	72.	(b)
41.	(b)	42.	(b)	43.	(c)	44.	(b)	73.	(a)	74.	(b)	75.	(a)	76.	(a)
45.	(a)	46.	(d)	47.	(d)	48.	(d)	77.	(b)	78.	(a)	79.	(b)	80.	(a)
49.	(c)	50.	(b)	51.	(a)	52.	(a)	81.	(a)	82.	(a)	83.	(a)	84.	(b)
53.	(b)	54.	(b)	55.	(a)	56.	(b)	85.	(a)	86.	(a)	87.	(b)	88.	(a)
57.	(a)	58.	(a)	59.	(b)	60.	(a)	89.	(b)	90.	(b)	91.	(b)	92.	(a)
61	(a)	62.	(a)	63.	(b)	64.	(a)	93.	(a)	94.	(a)	95.	(a)	96.	(a)
65.	(a)	66.	(b)	67.	(b)	68.	(a)	97.	(a)	98.	(a)	99.	(b)	100.	(b)

Model Test Paper XVIII

1. **To select nonadjacent files, press and hold the .... key while selecting individual files.**
   (a) Tab (b) Shift
   (c) Windows (d) Ctrl
2. **When a hacker penetrates a network, this is a network .... issue.**
   (a) Performance (b) Reliability
   (c) Security (d) None of above
3. **Output of the Calc expression is =500/10/2.**
   (a) 10 (b) 25
   (c) 50 (d) 200
4. **KYC means**
   (a) Know your character
   (b) Know your customer
   (c) Both of the above
   (d) None of the above
5. **To select a column the easiest method is to ....**
   (a) Drag from the top cell in the column to last cell in the column
   (b) Double-click any cell in the column
   (c) Ctrl+A
   (d) Click the column heading
6. **QR code stand for**
   (a) Quick Result Code
   (b) Quick Response Code
   (c) Quick Restore Code
   (d) None of the above
7. **Which social media is more based on image and video.**
   (a) Instagram (b) Facebook
   (c) Twitter (d) None of the above
8. **Viruses are ......**
   (a) Computer made (b) System made
   (c) Man made (d) None of the above
9. **A floppy disk contains.....**
   (a) Sectors only
   (b) Circular tracks only
   (c) Both circular tracks and sectors
   (d) None of the above
10. **Which key is used to insert a new worksheet.**
    (a) Shift+Alt+F1 (b) Shift+F11
    (c) Ctrl+F12 (d) Alt+F1
11. **Fourth Industrial revolution is based on the concept of the smart factory. Which type of development work have in this.**
    (a) Power (b) Electric work
    (c) Cyber physical production system
    (d) None of the above
12. **Technology which is used to provide internet by transmitting data over wires of telephone network is?**
    (a) Diodes (b) Transmitter
    (c) DSL (d) HHL
13. **Which one of these stores more data than a DVD?**
    (a) Floppy (b) CD Rom
    (c) Red Ray Disk (d) Blue Ray Disk
14. **In which of the following form, data is stored in computer?**
    (a) Binary (b) Decimal
    (c) Octal (d) HexaDecimal
15. **A happy face or sad face image placed in the message text of an email is called a(n) ....**
    (a) Charm (b) Emotion
    (c) Winkie (d) Facetile
16. **AEPS stands for.........**
    (a) Aadhaar E-Payment System
    (b) Aadhaar Enabled Payment System
    (c) Aadhaar Encashment Pyment System
    (d) None of above
17. **Screen that comes on when you turn on your computer that shows all the icons is called ....**
    (a) Smurfs (b) Carl
    (c) Desktop (d) Spreadsheet
18. **Coud computing save its data on ....**
    (a) Pen Drive (b) Internet
    (c) CD-ROM (d) Hard Disk
19. **If you receive an email message that includes multiple recipients, and you want to respond back to the same list of recipients, use the ....**
    (a) Forward All (b) Forward
    (c) Reply All (d) Reply
20. **Which of the following is anti-virus program**
    (a) K7 (b) Quick Heal
    (c) Norton (d) All of the above

21. **What is full form CMOS?**
(a) Complementary Metal Oxide Semiconductor
(b) Content Metal Oxide Semiconductor
(c) Complementary Metal Oscilator Semiconductor
(d) Complementary Metal Oxygen Semiconductor

22. **What is Atal Pension Yojana (APY)?**
(a) Encouraged workers to voluntarily save for their retirement
(b) Provides social security to the unorganized sector
(c) Fixed pension is paid on attaining the age of 60 years
(d) All of the above

23. **Which component of computer is considered as it Heart?**
(a) Keyboard (b) Monitor
(c) Microprocessor (d) Scanner

24. **In SMTP, the command to write receivers mail address is written with this command**
(a) Rcpt to (b) Send to
(c) Mail to (d) None of the above

25. **Documents, Movies, Images and Photographs etc are stored at:**
(a) Web Server (b) Application Server
(c) File Server (d) Print Server

26. **Which of the following is used in RAM?**
(a) Semi Conductor (b) Conductor
(c) Transistor (d) Vaccum Tubes

27. **Who was constituted as the father of Internet?**
(a) Vint Cerf (b) Charles Babbage
(c) Martin Cooper (d) Denis Riche

28. **USB is which type of storage device?**
(a) Secondary (b) Primary
(c) Tertiary (d) None of the above

29. **Who was the founder of Bluetooth?**
(a) Martin Cooper (b) Ericson
(c) Apple (d) Steve Jobs

30. **What is the name of first super computer of India?**
(a) Param 8000 (b) Saga 220
(c) Param 6000 (d) ENIAC

31. **What is the meaning of OSI, in term of computers?**
(a) Open System Intrerelation
(b) Open Software Intrerelation
(c) Open System Interconntion
(d) Open Software Interconnection

32. **What is meaning of EEPROM?**
(a) Electrical Erasable Programmable Read Only Memory
(b) Electronically Erasable Programmable Read Only Memory
(c) Erasable Program
(d) Electrically Erasable Program

33. **Full form of WORM**
(a) Write On Random Memory
(b) Write Once Read Many
(c) Work On Real Memory
(d) None of the above

34. **Which type of storage device is BIOS?**
(a) Secondary (b) Primary
(c) Tertiary (d) Not a storage device

35. **An electronic path that sends signals from one part of computer to another is:**
(a) Modem (b) Logic Gate
(c) Serial Port (d) Bus

36. **Full form of SBI is ....**
(a) Bank of India (b) State Bank of India
(c) Stock Bank of India (d) None of the above

37. **In banking, railways, which computers are used?**
(a) Micro Computers (b) Mini Computers
(c) Super Computers (d) Main Frames

38. **ARP stands for?**
(a) Address Resolution Protocol
(b) Address Reserve Protocol
(c) Address Recording Protocol
(d) Address Representative Protocol

39. **What can be considered as basic building blocks of a digital circuit?**
(a) Diode (b) Logic Gate
(c) CMOS (d) Semi Conductor

40. **Who invented keyboard?**
(a) Steve Jobs (b) James Gosling
(c) Christopher Latham Sholes
(d) Martin Cooper

41. **Which program is run by BIOS to check hardware components are working properly while computer is turned ON?**
(a) POST (b) DMOS
(c) RIP (d) CMOS

42. **With the email we can attach .... number of file:**
(a) Not more than two
(b) Not more than five

(c) Both (a) and (b)
(d) None of these

43. The communication protocol used by Internet is:
(a) TELNET (b) HTTP
(c) TCP/IP (d) UTP

44. Maximum amount we can write on Cheque....
(a) No Limit (b) Rs. 100 crore
(c) Rs. 1 crore (d) None of the above

45. Which of the following suppors for Big data analytics?
(a) Social Network (b) Cloud Storage
(c) E-Commerce (d) All of the above

46. What is full form of TIFF?
(a) Tagged Image File Format
(b) The Image File Format
(c) The Image Fax Format
(d) Tagged Image File Front

47. MIME stands for:
(a) Multipurpose Internet Mail Email
(b) Multipurpose Internet Mail Extensions
(c) Multipurpose International Mail End
(d) Multipurpose Internation Mail Entity

48. A user can get files from another computer on the Internet by using:
(a) TELNET (b) HTTP
(c) FTP (d) UTP

49. Simple mail transfer protocol (SMTP) utilizes ..... as the transport layer protocol for electronic mail transfer.
(a) UDP (b) TCP
(c) SCTP (d) DCCP

50. SMTP is used to deliver message to
(a) User's mailbox (b) User's terminal
(c) Both (a) and (b)
(d) None of the mentioned

51. 'UMANG' means Unified Mobile Application for New-age Governance, thrugh this App anyone an access E-Governance Services on Mobile.
(a) True (b) False

52. Hypertext contains linked of any file.
(a) True (b) False

53. In instant messaging as one user types a message on one computer, the same message appears on a recipient's computer at the same time.
(a) True (b) False

54. Format painter facility is available in Calc like Libre-Office Writer.
(a) True (b) False

55. Maximum number of columns in a Calc Sheet is AMJ.
(a) True (b) False

56. Window menu allows you to work with two documents simultaneously.
(a) True (b) False

57. Bold character are thicker than regular characters.
(a) True (b) False

58. A dynamic document is created by a web server whenever a browser requests the document.
(a) True (b) False

59. Bullets and numbering appears in "view" menu in LibreOffice Impress.
(a) True (b) False

60. E-mail address are case-sensitive.
(a) True (b) False

61. A protocol used for fetching e-mail from a mailbox is POP3.
(a) True (b) False

62. Set stand for Secure Electronic Transactions
(a) True (b) False

63. Bullets and Numbering appears in the standard toolbar in LibreOffice writer.
(a) True (b) False

64. Rules for exchanging data between computers are called Protocols.
(a) True (b) False

65. A bus is a common pathway through which information is connected from one component to another.
(a) True (b) False

66. ALU is used to store data.
(a) True (b) False

67. Programs that automatically submit your search request to several search engines simultaneously are called meta search engine.
(a) True (b) False

68. Unwanted and Unsolicited mails are called Spam.
(a) True (b) False

69. Communication is the most popular internet activity.
(a) True (b) False

70. Many individuals create their own personal sites called Web logs, or blogs.
(a) True (b) False

71. **E-mail can be used to send broadcast message, but only within your own company.**
(a) True (b) False

72. **E-mail is limited to text based messages.**
(a) True (b) False

73. **Hypertext is also known as hyperlink.**
(a) True (b) False

74. **A video of 60 second can be recorded and send through instagram.**
(a) True (b) False

75. **LibreOffice Impres support maximum zooming upto 3000%**
(a) True (b) False

76. **Even and odd pages can have different footers in LibreOffice writer.**
(a) True (b) False

77. **The favourites feature of Internet Explorer allows you to save the URLs of Web pages you visit frequently.**
(a) True (b) False

78. **From an e-mail address, one can find out the domain name, where this e-mail address is hosted.**
(a) True (b) False

79. **Refresh button returns to home page.**
(a) True (b) False

80. **All incoming e-mail messages are to be stored in the OUTBOX folder.**
(a) True (b) False

81. **A protocol used for fetching e-mail from a mailbox is POP1.**
(a) True (b) False

82. **The request for Comments (RFCs) core topics are Internet and the TCP/IP protocol suites.**
(a) True (b) False

83. **DNS is a distributed database offering strong consistency and atomicity guarantees.**
(a) True (b) False

84. **Lycos is an internet search engine and web portal.**
(a) True (b) False

85. **F8 is the keyboard shortcut used for spell checking a document.**
(a) True (b) False

86. **When you copy a formula in LibreOffice Calc, absolute cell references do not change.**
(a) True (b) False

87. **An absolute cell reference**
(a) True (b) False

88. **In LibreOffice Calc, pressing [Ctrl] + [Spacebar] select the entire column.**
(a) True (b) False

89. **Web browser lets you to download only while surfing the Internet.**
(a) True (b) False

90. **A set of rules is known as protocol.**
(a) True (b) False

91. **E-commerce primarily consists of the distributing, buying, selling, marketing, and servicing of products or services over electronic systems such as the Internet.**
(a) True (b) False

92. **News groups are also known as usenet.**
(a) True (b) False

93. **DNS provides maping of IP with domain name.**
(a) True (b) False

94. **The Internet is a collection of files.**
(a) True (b) False

95. **[Shift+F7] key is used for Thesaurus in LibreOffice.**
(a) True (b) False

96. **The full form of ISP is Information Source Provider.**
(a) True (b) False

97. **A blog is a website where entries are made in journal style and displayed in a reserve chronological order.**
(a) True (b) False

98. **Firewall is a network security system that monitors and controls incoming and outgoing network traffic based on predetermined security rules.**
(a) True (b) False

99. **In dialup connection, you can connect your computer to an ISP Server, with the help of modem.**
(a) True (b) False

100. **First page of website is known as home page.**
(a) True (b) False

Answers

1.	(d)	2.	(c)	3.	(b)	4.	(b)
5.	(d)	6.	(b)	7.	(a)	8.	(d)
9.	(c)	10.	(a)	11.	(d)	12.	(c)
13.	(d)	14.	(a)	15.	(b)	16.	(b)
17.	(c)	18.	(b)	19.	(c)	20.	(d)

21. (a) 22. (d) 23. (c) 24. (a)
25. (c) 26. (a) 27. (a) 28. (c)
29. (b) 30. (a) 31. (c) 32. (a)
33. (b) 34. (b) 35. (b) 36. (b)
37. (d) 38. (a) 39. (b) 40. (c)
41. (a) 42. (d) 43. (c) 44. (a)
45. (d) 46. (a) 47. (b) 48. (c)
49. (b) 50. (c) 51. (a) 52. (a)
53. (a) 54. (a) 55. (a) 56. (a)
57. (a) 58. (a) 59. (b) 60. (b)
61 (a) 62. (a) 63. (a) 64. (a)
65. (a) 66. (b) 67. (a) 68. (a)
69. (a) 70. (a) 71. (b) 72. (b)
73. (b) 74. (a) 75. (a) 76. (a)
77. (a) 78. (a) 79. (b) 80. (b)
81. (b) 82. (a) 83. (a) 84. (a)
85. (b) 86. (a) 87. (a) 88. (a)
89. (a) 90. (a) 91. (a) 92. (b)
93. (a) 94. (b) 95. (a) 96. (b)
97. (a) 98. (a) 99. (a) 100. (a)

Model Test Paper XIX

1. **In which menu change case command appears:**
   (a) Slide Show (b) Insert
   (c) Edit (d) Format
2. **To read an E-mail, you need to .... with the E-mail Service.**
   (a) Register (b) Sign Up
   (c) Sign In (d) None of these
3. **Following is the example of Toggle case**
   (a) Toggle case (b) TOGGLE CASE
   (c) tOGGLE cASE (d) None of these
4. **CC in the email stands for:**
   (a) Carbon Copy (b) Crease Copy
   (c) Cyber Copy (d) None of the above
5. **........ is program designed to destroy data on your computer and "infect" other computer.**
   (a) Torpado (b) Virus
   (c) Disease (d) Hurican
6. **Alignment buttons are available on the .... toolbar of LibreOffice Writer.**
   (a) Formatting Toolbar (b) Status Bar
   (c) Standard Toolbar (d) None of these
7. **......... is a method of exchanging digital message usally over Internet or network.**
   (a) POST (b) E-mail
   (c) E-Data (d) Digital Message
8. **Which of the following method is correct for securing your computer.**
   (a) Using and Enabling Firewall
   (b) System Updating
   (c) Using Antivirus Program
   (d) All of the above
9. **Which of these domains is restricted to commercial purpose?**
   (a) .org (b) .com
   (c) .edu (d) .net
10. **LibreOffice Impress, slide sorter command is found under which menu.**
    (a) Tools (b) File
    (c) Edit (d) View
11. **Which of the following can you use to add time to the slides in a LibreOffice Impress.**
    (a) Slide show menu (b) Slide layout
    (c) Rehearse timings button
    (d) Slide transition button
12. **Which of the following is the largest unit of storage?**
    (a) TB (b) MB
    (c) KB (d) GB
13. **In which year NEFT services has been started?**
    (a) 2002 (b) 2005
    (c) 1999 (d) 2009
14. **IPO cycle stands for ....**
    (a) Integrated Programme Onboard
    (b) Input Process Output
    (c) Integrated Process Output
    (d) Input Program Onboard
15. **Internet is......**
    (a) Decentralized System
    (b) Complex System
    (c) Dynamic System
    (d) All of the above
16. **Pan card is valid only for?**
    (a) Deposit in Bank
    (b) Only ID for Card Holders
    (c) None of these
    (d) All of the above
17. **You a new presentation in impress by using the following options except.**
    (a) Click on New Icon (b) Ctrl+N
    (c) Ctrl+O
    (d) File menu > New Presentation
18. **Which of the following key is used to start slide show from current slide in LibreOffice Impress.**
    (a) Alt+F5 (b) Ctrl+F5
    (c) Ctrl+F7 (d) Shift+F5
19. **Which is not a type of trust seal?**
    (a) Security Seal (b) Privacy Seal
    (c) Business Seal (d) Personal Seal
20. **Under which menu page setup appears.**
    (a) File Menu (b) Tools Menu
    (c) Slide Show Menu (d) None of these
21. **If you want to copy a selection of text, which button do you click?**
    (a) Copy (b) Move
    (c) Cut (d) Duplicate

22. Short cut used for print preview LibreOffice Calc and Impress is:
(a) Ctrl+P (b) Ctrl+O
(c) Ctrl+Shift+O (d) Ctrl+F

23. The software used to view web pages on the www is ....
(a) Web Browser (b) Web Reader
(c) Web Server (d) None of these

24. Which of the following is a GRAPHICAL PACKAGE?
(a) MS Excel (b) Coral Draw
(c) MS Word (d) None of these

25. The default name of the Impress Presentation is ......
(a) Slide 1 (b) Calc
(c) Untitled 1 - LibreOffice Impress
(d) Writer

26. Internet traffic is also known as
(a) Consession (b) Confection
(c) Concaitnation (d) Conjunction

27. The most common input device used today is:
(a) CPU (b) Motherboard
(c) System Unit (d) Keyboard

28. GUI means Graphical User Interface and is used as an interface between:
(a) Main and Machine
(b) Hardware and Software
(c) Hardware and User
(d) None of these

29. In computer terminology, information means
(a) Data (b) Digit
(c) Program (d) Alphanumeric Data

30. A collection of eight bits is called:
(a) Word (b) Byte
(c) File (d) Record

31. Graphic objects can be inserted into word through.
(a) From File (b) Clip Art
(c) Chart (d) All of the above

32. UPI Interface is governed by
(a) SBI (b) RBI
(c) Finance Ministry (d) None of above

33. Netscape navigator is a
(a) Browser (b) Website
(c) E-mail Programme (d) All of above

34. Which is the largest commercial bank in India?
(a) HDFC (b) SBI
(c) Central Bank of India
(d) ICICI

35. When LibreOffice Writer gets loaded, the opening screen displays a document named:
(a) Document (b) Untitled 1
(c) Display of Document Name
(d) Doc 1

36. The Save As, dialog box can be used to:
(a) Save the file for other name
(b) First time save of file
(c) Save the file for other format as MS Word
(d) All of above

37. To delete the selected sentences, we can press the following key:
(a) Backspace (b) Del
(c) Both (a) and (b) (d) None of these

38. Which device is used as the standard pointing device in a Graphical User Environment?
(a) Mouse (b) Keyboard
(c) Track Ball (d) Joystick

39. This is a element of 3D Processing.
(a) Laser Melting (b) CAD
(c) Both (a) and (b) (d) All of the above

40. The Central Processing Unit (CPU) consists of .....
(a) Input, Output and Processing
(b) Control Unit, Processing and Primary Collection
(c) Control Unit, Arithmetic Suggestion Unit and Secondary Collection
(d) Conrol Unit, Arithmetical Suggestion Unit and Register

41. Outlook express is a.........
(a) Search Engine (b) Browser
(c) E-mail Client (d) Editor

42. Fixed deposits and recurring deposits are ....
(a) Repayable after in agreed period
(b) Repayable on demand
(c) Repayable after death of depositors
(d) Non Repayable

43. Formatting toolbar has lot of buttons that you can quickly apply to numerical data on the Calc worksheet. These buttons are:
(a) Percent Style (b) Currency Style
(c) Coma Style (d) All of the above

44. Which mobile wallet does not permit cash withdrawal.
(a) Semi Open Wallet (b) Open Wallet

(c) Semi Closed Wallet (d) None of these

45. **You can logged in remote computer through:**
(a) FTP (b) Telnet
(c) HTTP (d) None of these

46. **The combination of the column letter and row number for a cell in an Calc spreadsheet is called:**
(a) Cell Identification Number
(b) Cell Across
(c) Cell Identify
(d) Cell Reference

47. **<TD>.....</TD> tag is used for ......**
(a) Table Heading (b) Table Data
(c) Table Dimension (d) Table Row

48. **IP addresses are converted to:**
(a) One Alphanumeric Strings
(b) One Binary String
(c) One Hexadecimal String
(d) One Series in Domain Name

49. **News Servers utilize ...... to distribute documents to readers.**
(a) News (b) NNTP
(c) FTP (d) HTTP

50. **<script> tags can be placed with in ....**
(a) Body (b) Head
(c) Both (a) and (b) (d) None of the above

51. **Peer to Peer networking means that you have a central server, to which all computers in the network are directly connected.**
(a) True (b) False

52. **Ctrl+F2 shortcut key is used to insert function.**
(a) True (b) False

53. **HTML is similar to search engine.**
(a) True (b) False

54. **DigiLocker is a service launched by Government of India in February 2015 to provide a secure dedicated personal electronic space for storing the documents of resident Indian citizens.**
(a) True (b) False

55. **Pie chart can represent multiple series of data.**
(a) True (b) False

56. **ECB stand for External Commercial Borrowings.**
(a) True (b) False

57. **You can write =A1/A2 for divide the value of A1 and A2.**
(a) True (b) False

58. **When you create a formula that contains a function, the insert function dialog box helps you to enter worksheet functions.**
(a) True (b) False

59. **You can have a different header and footer on each sheet of a workbook.**
(a) True (b) False

60. **In LibreOffice Calc you can count the number of entries in a column or a row using the Count () function.**
(a) True (b) False

61. **Google cardboard is the example of artificial intelligence.**
(a) True (b) False

62. **Digital Signature is same as a scanned signature.**
(a) True (b) False

63. **You can preview a template before choosing it.**
(a) True (b) False

64. **An organization chart is used to illustrate hierarchical relationships.**
(a) True (b) False

65. **UPI, AEPS and USSD is a digital payment system developed by NPCI.**
(a) True (b) False

66. **The first time you save a LibreOffice Impress presentation, you must name it.**
(a) True (b) False

67. **You cannot change the Font style of the entire workbook by a single command. It can change only worksheet by worksheet.**
(a) True (b) False

68. **LibreOffice Calc ignores manual page breaks when you use the Fit to option of the page setup.**
(a) True (b) False

69. **Nine menu are found in LibreOffice Calc.**
(a) True (b) False

70. **Press (PgUp) to move to the next slide.**
(a) True (b) False

71. **POS - (Point of Sale) terminal is a digital device.**
(a) True (b) False

72. **Multiuser is a generic term for the use of two or more central processing units (CPUs) within a single computer system.**
(a) True (b) False

73. **Check boxes are used to present options requiring individual on/off decisions in Message boxes.**
(a) True (b) False

74. **LibreOffice Impress templates have .odt extension.**
(a) True (b) False

75. **To use a computer you need an operating system.**
(a) True (b) False

76. **FTP servers store files that you can transfer to or from your computer.**
(a) True (b) False

77. **Hiring leased lines is cheaper than a dial-up connection on the Internet.**
(a) True (b) False

78. **All conversations on the IPC, are in English.**
(a) True (b) False

79. **Cookies store information about the web pages in your favorites list.**
(a) True (b) False

80. **The normal view has three working areas: one the left, outline tab and slides tab; on the right, the slide pane; and on the bottom, the notes pane.**
(a) True (b) False

81. **LibreOffice Writer template does not include style formatting.**
(a) True (b) False

82. **The first character has to be underscored or letter when defining a name of a cell or range of cells.**
(a) True (b) False

83. **The spelling and grammar check can only be done on the text selected.**
(a) True (b) False

84. **In web site designing you should make the title catchy, descriptive and accurate.**
(a) True (b) False

85. **Headers and footers are displayed in the normal view of LibreOffice Writer.**
(a) True (b) False

86. **In a multi-page document, the dotted line that extends on a page is called as soft page break.**
(a) True (b) False

87. **As you scroll in a document, the insertion point also moves.**
(a) True (b) False

88. **Auto Text can be used to insert graphics that you use frequently in the document.**
(a) True (b) False

89. **You can not use different page-numbering styles in different section of your document.**
(a) True (b) False

90. **In writer, an hypen is the last line of paragraph that appears at the top of a page.**
(a) True (b) False

91. **Pressing (Home) moves the active cell to column A of the current row.**
(a) True (b) False

92. **From the Mail Merge Helper dialog box, you can only open an existing data sources but cannot create a new one.**
(a) True (b) False

93. **Kelbin systrom and Mike Krizer are founder of Instagram.**
(a) True (b) False

94. **B2B, B2C and C2C are a type of E-commerce.**
(a) True (b) False

95. **Selecting the Autofit selection option, automatically adjusts the width of the column to the maximum width entry.**
(a) True (b) False

96. **NEFT Timing is morning 8 am to evening 7 pm.**
(a) True (b) False

97. **Using LAN you can connect various computers.**
(a) True (b) False

98. **The distance from the top of the page to your insertion point is displayed in the Status bar of the document.**
(a) True (b) False

99. **Styles can be used to generate a table of contents quickly in LibreOffice Writer.**
(a) True (b) False

100. **HTML is used for creating home page for World Wide Web.**
(a) True (b) False

Answers

1.	(d)	2.	(c)	3.	(c)	4.	(a)
5.	(b)	6.	(a)	7.	(b)	8.	(d)
9.	(b)	10.	(d)	11.	(d)	12.	(a)
13.	(b)	14.	(b)	15.	(d)	16.	(b)
17.	(a)	18.	(d)	19.	(d)	20.	(d)
21.	(a)	22.	(b)	23.	(a)	24.	(b)
25.	(c)	26.	(d)	27.	(d)	28.	(c)
29.	(a)	30.	(b)	31.	(d)	32.	(b)
33.	(a)	34.	(b)	35.	(b)	36.	(d)
37.	(c)	38.	(a)	39.	(c)	40.	(d)

41.	(c)	42.	(a)	43.	(d)	44.	(c)
45.	(b)	46.	(d)	47.	(b)	48.	(d)
49.	(b)	50.	(c)	51.	(b)	52.	(a)
53.	(b)	54.	(a)	55.	(b)	56.	(a)
57.	(a)	58.	(a)	59.	(a)	60.	(a)
61	(b)	62.	(b)	63.	(a)	64.	(a)
65.	(a)	66.	(a)	67.	(a)	68.	(a)
69.	(a)	70.	(b)	71.	(a)	72.	(b)
73.	(a)	74.	(a)	75.	(a)	76.	(a)
77.	(b)	78.	(a)	79.	(a)	80.	(a)
81.	(b)	82.	(b)	83.	(b)	84.	(a)
85.	(b)	86.	(a)	87.	(b)	88.	(b)
89.	(b)	90.	(b)	91.	(a)	92.	(b)
93.	(a)	94.	(a)	95.	(a)	96.	(a)
97.	(a)	98.	(a)	99.	(a)	100.	(a)

Model Test Paper XX

1. **Operating System manages?**
   (a) I/O Devices (b) Memory
   (c) Processor (d) All of the options
2. **Which of the following displays the contents of the active cell?**
   (a) Active Cell (b) Name Box
   (c) Formula Bar (d) Menu Bar
3. **Printer is:**
   (a) Data (b) Software
   (c) Hardware (d) None of the above
4. **KYC means.**
   (a) Know your character
   (b) Know y our customer
   (c) Both of the above
   (d) None of the above
5. **Which of the following is used as Operating Systems for Mobile Phone and Tablets**
   (a) MKDIR Androids OS
   (b) Windows OS
   (c) iOS
   (d) All of above
6. **Below all are the examples of real security and privacy threats except.**
   (a) Worm (b) Hackers
   (c) Virus (d) Spam
7. **The maximum limit of attachment in Outlook and G-Mail are....**
   (a) 20 & 25 MB (b) 25 & 35 MB
   (c) Both (a) and (b) (d) 50 & 55 MB
8. **Which of the following is not an external threat to the computer or computer network.**
   (a) Crackers (b) Adware
   (c) Trojan Horses (d) None of the above
9. **A(n) .... search is a search whose hits are restricted to Web pages within the current Web site.**
   (a) Exploratory (b) Hierarchical
   (c) Site (d) Global
10. **A blockchain is a growing list of records, which work on the basis of:**
    (a) Virtual Reality (b) Robotics
    (c) Cryptographic (d) None of the above
11. **A double sided magnetic disk has six disks normally uses .... surface for this pack.**
    (a) 6 (b) 9
    (c) 10 (d) 12
12. **The most important system software of computer is the:**
    (a) Operating System
    (b) Microprocessor
    (c) Application Software
    (d) Automation Software
13. **UNIVAC is ....**
    (a) Unvalued Automatic Computer
    (b) Universal Automatic Computer
    (c) Universal Array Computer
    (d) Unique Automatic Computer
14. **IPV4 address is of how many bits:**
    (a) 5 bits (b) 16 bits
    (c) 32 bits (d) 64 bits
15. **DVD is based on:**
    (a) Magnetic Disk Technology
    (b) USB Pen Technology
    (c) Optical Disk Technology
    (d) Media to store Video data only
16. **Which of the following is not windows e-mail programme?**
    (a) Outlook (b) Eudora
    (c) Pegasus (d) Pine
17. **The .... protocol has features that allow uploading of mail messages:**
    (a) IMAP (b) SNMP
    (c) HTTP (d) POP3
18. **Which of the following does not have word processing?**
    (a) OpenOffice (b) Google Docs
    (c) Google Chrome (d) MS Office
19. **........ is the result produce by a computer.**
    (a) Memory (b) Data
    (c) Input (d) Output
20. **Route redistribution is the process of introducing external routes into an .... network.**
    (a) BGP (b) EGP
    (c) Hybrid (d) OSPF
21. **IBM 1401 is**
    (a) Second Generation Computer

(b) First Generation Computer
(c) Fourth Generation Computer
(d) Third Generation Computer

22. What is validity period of cheque?
(a) 3 months from date of issue
(b) 4 months from date of issue
(c) Unlimited
(d) 1 month from date of issue

23. When was the world's first laptop computer introduced in the market and by whom?
(a) Epson, 1981
(b) Hewlett-Packard
(c) Tandy model-2000, 1985
(d) Lap link travelling software Inc. 1982

24. Access time is:
(a) Seek Time
(b) Seek Time + Latency Time
(c) Latency Time (d) Seek Time

25. CAD stands for:
(a) Computer Alogrithm for Design
(b) Computer Aided Design
(c) Computer Application in Design
(d) All of the above

26. Which layer of International Standard Organization OSI model is responsible for creating and recognizing frame boundaries?
(a) Physical Layer (b) Data-Link Layer
(c) Network Layer (d) Transport Layer

27. Which of the following choices is not available in the "select a category" drop down menu of the Insert Function dialog box?
(a) Macro (b) Information
(c) Text (d) User Defined

28. For a browser to connect to other resources, the location or address of the resources must be specified. These addresses are called:
(a) Packets (b) E-mail Forms
(c) MSN (d) URLs

29. Extension of Calc spreadsheet file is:
(a) .XXL (b) .odx
(c) .ods (d) None of the above

30. POS means:
(a) Point of Supervision (b) Present of Sale
(c) Point of Sale (d) None of the above

31. Operating system is used in.....
(a) Smart Card (b) ATM Card
(c) Microwave Oven (d) Computer System

32. Port number for SMTP protocol is ....
(a) 25 (b) 22
(c) 80 (d) 110

33. Which of the following methods can be used to enter data in a cell?
(a) Clicking on the formula bar
(b) Pressing an arrow
(c) Pressing the Tab (d) All of the above

34. WAIS stands for
(a) Wide Area Internet Service
(b) Wide Area Information Servers
(c) Wide Area Information System
(d) None of the above

35. Sending a file from your personal computer's memory or disk to another computer is called:
(a) Uploading (b) Logging
(c) Hanging (d) Downloading

36. Display wheel printer is a type of:
(a) Impact Printer (b) Matrix Priner
(c) Manual Printer (d) Laser Printer

37. Magnetic disks are the most popular medium for
(a) Sequential access (b) Direct access
(c) Both (a) and (b) (d) None of the above

38. Which of the following is used for calculation work.
(a) Mouse (b) CU
(c) CPU (d) ALU

39. Which of the following is a search engine?
(a) Google (b) Bing & Yahoo
(c) Lycos (d) All of the above

40. Who built the world's first electronic calculator using telephone relays, light bulbs and batteries.
(a) Konrard Zues (b) Claude shannon
(c) Howard H Aiken (d) George Stibits

41. A bit of text that automatically inserted at the bottom of every sent message is known as:
(a) Signature
(b) Personal level indicator
(c) People widget
(d) People text

42. HTM is an acronym for:
(a) Hyperlink Markup
(b) Hypertext Modem
(c) Hypertext Markup Language
(d) Hypertext Markup Link

43. Which of the following method is right to secure your mobile.

(a) Passcode (b) App Lock

(c) Use two factor authentication

(d) All of the aboe

44. Skypee is one of the best.....

(a) Internet Telephony (b) Web Browser

(c) Protocol (d) Web Server

45. For your E-mail, PGP allows you to:

(a) Encrypt (b) Enhanced

(c) Design (d) Decrypt

46. Aadhar is:

(a) Identity proof issued by UIDAI

(b) 12 digit number card

(c) Both 12 digit number card & Identity proof issued by UIDAI

(d) None of the above

47. We can delete the maximum number of e-mail at a time is:

(a) Only Two (b) Multiple

(c) Only Three (d) Only One

48. The World Wide Web is composed of:

(a) Only 100 Web Pages

(b) 1 Page

(c) Millions of Web Pages

(d) 500 Web Pages

49. Which of the following is the type of cyber security?

(a) Phishing (b) Malware

(c) Rensomware (d) All of the above

50. Which type of the fonts are best suit to display large amount of the text?

(a) Sans series font (b) Text font

(c) Picture font (d) Serif font

51. In LibreOffice Calc, If we write formula =3+4*5 then result is 35, but =(3+4)*5 then result is 23.

(a) True (b) False

52. A file which contains readymade styles that you can use for your LibreOffice Impress presentations is called Template.

(a) True (b) False

53. Search Engine maintain heavy database of keywords and URL's?

(a) True (b) False

54. Port number for IMAP protocol is 143.

(a) True (b) False

55. Cylinder, cone, and pyramid are all charts types in LibreOffice.

(a) True (b) False

56. A web browser is a software program that allows you to browse, search and receive various types of information such as websites, images, video and audio files and other documents on the web.

(a) True (b) False

57. The uniform resources locator (URL) is a standard for specifying any kind of information on the internet.

(a) True (b) False

58. Hardware is the physical structure of computer and software refers the programs needed for computer to perform jobs.

(a) True (b) False

59. Google pay are mobile wallet.

(a) True (b) False

60. The full form NABARD is National Bank for Agricultue and Rural Development.

(a) True (b) False

61. Shortcut of Hyperlink is Ctrl+K in LibreOffice.

(a) True (b) False

62. In LibreOffice Impress Pressing Esc key during the slide show ends the presentation.

(a) True (b) False

63. Security in e-commerce means protecting an organization's data resources from unauthorized access.

(a) True (b) False

64. To switch back to receiving individual messages, send the message set list digests.

(a) True (b) False

65. Optical mouse uses tiny camera to detect movement.

(a) True (b) False

66. System bus is used to connect CPU to a central switch.

(a) True (b) False

67. LibreOffice Calc provides an AutoCalculate feature which by default, will display the SUM of values in a selected range.

(a) True (b) False

68. Back button in a Browser is used to visit the previoous page that referred you to the page you are currently located at.

(a) True (b) False

69. FTP is File Transfer Procedure.

(a) True (b) False

70. **A firewall is as a part of a router program filters packets travelling from and to the intranet from the internet.**
(a) True (b) False

71. **One of the options available to the presenter during a slide show in Impress is Transitions.**
(a) True (b) False

72. **In LibreOffice Writer, the easiest way to resize a picture is by dragging its edges to match the size and shape you want.**
(a) True (b) False

73. **Because of Increasing IM Integration in Popular Applications, IM networks are particularly vulnerable to a worm attack.**
(a) True (b) False

74. **AEPS means Aadhaar Enabled Payment System which requires Aadhar for authentication.**
(a) True (b) False

75. **BHIM means Bharat Interface for Money is a digital payment system launched on 30.12.2016.**
(a) True (b) False

76. **Presentation designs regulate the formatting and layout for the slide and are commonly called placeholders.**
(a) True (b) False

77. **The email message window is used to compose and send an email message.**
(a) True (b) False

78. **Ctrl-F performs same operation in LibreOffice Writer and LibreOffice Calc.**
(a) True (b) False

79. **A blank cell has the numeric value of blank.**
(a) True (b) False

80. **The two dimensional representation of an image is known as image resolution.**
(a) True (b) False

81. **ISDN is an example of circuit switched network.**
(a) True (b) False

82. **To start pine, program, choose the option from the menu by pressing <L> and <Enter>.**
(a) True (b) False

83. **OTP (One Time Password) is used for safe login and safe online transfer of money.**
(a) True (b) False

84. **GUI Operating Systems are much easier for end-users to learn and use because commands do not need to be memorize.**
(a) True (b) False

85. **As per email netiquette, one should not store large amounts of old mail that you no longer need.**
(a) True (b) False

86. **Sent item/sent box is the box where copies of sent message saved.**
(a) True (b) False

87. **Two persons can have same email address.**
(a) True (b) False

88. **IMPS Stand for Immediate Payment Service.**
(a) True (b) False

89. **The FTP protocol is the client/server program used to retrieve the document.**
(a) True (b) False

90. **[Ctrl] + [End] moves the last cell containing contents in the LibreOffice Calc Spreadhseet.**
(a) True (b) False

91. **Ctrl+A method will select the full page open.**
(a) True (b) False

92. **Classifying content in social media happens through an activity such as tagging.**
(a) True (b) False

93. **To deliver a message to the correct application program running on a host, the port address must be consulted.**
(a) True (b) False

94. **Facebook is social networking site.**
(a) True (b) False

95. **To organize you bookmarks menu into sections, add separators.**
(a) True (b) False

96. **Left Key of mouse is used to open Pop-up Menu.**
(a) True (b) False

97. **Data can be transmitted by using the OSI model.**
(a) True (b) False

98. **Telnet service enables an Internet user to log in to another computer on the internet from his/her local computer.**
(a) True (b) False

99. **Maximum size of a page in most word processors is limited to 22 inch x 22**
(a) True (b) False

100. **When responding to posts, you should only say things that you would be willing to say when you meet with them face to face.**
(a) True (b) False

Answers

1.	(d)	2.	(c)	3.	(d)	4.	(b)
5.	(d)	6.	(d)	7.	(a)	8.	(d)
9.	(c)	10.	(c)	11.	(c)	12.	(a)
13.	(b)	14.	(b)	15.	(c)	16.	(d)
17.	(a)	18.	(c)	19.	(d)	20.	(d)
21.	(a)	22.	(a)	23.	(a)	24.	(b)
25.	(b)	26.	(b)	27.	(a)	28.	(d)
29.	(c)	30.	(b)	31.	(d)	32.	(a)
33.	(d)	34.	(b)	35.	(a)	36.	(a)
37.	(c)	38.	(d)	39.	(d)	40.	(d)
41.	(a)	42.	(d)	43.	(d)	44.	(a)
45.	(a)	46.	(c)	47.	(b)	48.	(c)
49.	(d)	50.	(d)	51.	(b)	52.	(a)
53.	(a)	54.	(a)	55.	(a)	56.	(a)
57.	(a)	58.	(a)	59.	(a)	60.	(a)
61	(a)	62.	(a)	63.	(a)	64.	(a)
65.	(a)	66.	(a)	67.	(b)	68.	(a)
69.	(b)	70.	(a)	71.	(a)	72.	(a)
73.	(a)	74.	(a)	75.	(a)	76.	(b)
77.	(a)	78.	(a)	79.	(b)	80.	(a)
81.	(a)	82.	(a)	83.	(a)	84.	(a)
85.	(a)	86.	(a)	87.	(b)	88.	(a)
89.	(b)	90.	(a)	91.	(a)	92.	(a)
93.	(b)	94.	(a)	95.	(a)	96.	(b)
97.	(a)	98.	(a)	99.	(a)	100.	(a)

Model Test Paper XXI

1. **UTS means Unreserved Ticketing System through App launched in ....**
   (a) February 2019 (b) January 2018
   (c) January 2019 (d) None of above
2. **Which is not a valid resolution of a screen?**
   (a) 1064 x 768 (b) 300 x 400
   (c) 1280 x 1024 (d) 800 x 600
3. **IPv4 address is a .... address that uniquely and universally defines the connection of a device (for example, a computer or a router) to the internet.**
   (a) 128 bit (b) 32 bit
   (c) 62 bit (d) 48 bit
4. **The word length of a computer is measured in ....**
   (a) Millimetres (b) Meters
   (c) Bytes (d) Bits
5. **Maximum Zoom in Impress are:**
   (a) 300% (b) 400%
   (c) 500% (d) 3000%
6. **Which one of the following is used to make secure transaction during net banking.**
   (a) Quick Result Code
   (b) OTP- one time password
   (c) Pin Number (d) None of above
7. **Most of the antivirus software works against:**
   (a) Only those viruses already known when the software is written.
   (b) Any virus except those in wireless communication application.
   (c) Any Virus
   (d) Only those viruses active on the Internet and through e-mail.
8. **In LibreOffice Impress, what combinations of commands are used for copy and paste?**
   (a) Invoke find dialog box
   (b) Ctrl+X and Ctrl+P
   (c) Ctrl+C and Ctrl+V
   (d) Ctrl+X and Ctrl+S
9. **The Domain Name System (DNS) associates a mail server to a domain with .... resource records containing the domain name of a host providing MTA services.**
   (a) Mail Transfer (b) Mail Send
   (c) Mail Exchange (d) Mail Transport
10. **Every web document has a unique addresses, what is it called?**
    (a) Domain
    (b) IP Address
    (c) Hyperlink
    (d) Universal Resource Locator
11. **Which technique react like humans.**
    (a) Artificial Intelligence
    (b) Big data analytics
    (c) Virtual Reality
    (d) None of the above
12. **When you delete a message from the Inbox:**
    (a) It is moved to the Deleted items folder.
    (b) The sender's name is deleted from your Contacts as well
    (c) it is moved to a holding area on the desktop or the Start screen
    (d) It is immediately permanently deleted
13. **Digital signature develop two types of key one Private key and seond .... that are mathematically linked.**
    (a) Cryptographic Key (b) Algorithm Key
    (c) Public Key (d) All of the above
14. **Which among the following is responsible for finding and loading operating system into RAM?**
    (a) CMOS (b) Bootstrap Loader
    (c) BIOS (d) DMOS
15. **XML stands for:**
    (a) Excellent Mark-up Links
    (b) Extended Mrking Links
    (c) Extra Mark-up Language
    (d) Extensible Mark-up Language
16. **Which of the following is not a transmission medium?**
    (a) Coaxial Cables (b) Microwave System
    (c) Modem (d) Telephone Line
17. **Shortcut Key to Copy in LibreOffice Writer is:**
    (a) Ctrl+Shift+C (b) Alt+C
    (c) Ctrl+C (d) None
18. **Which of the below is not tool for instant messaging.**
    (a) ZapTXT (b) Wikipedia
    (c) Yahoo Messangers (d) Zimbie

19. **Which of the following is related to mobile payment service.**
    (a) UPI (b) BHIM
    (c) Both (a) and (b) (d) None of the above
20. **....... is used for calculating and comparing.**
    (a) Modem (b) ALU
    (c) Disk Unit (d) Control Unit
21. **MDA stands for ....**
    (a) Mail Dissemination Agent
    (b) Mail Delivery Agent
    (c) Mail Dispatch Assurance
    (d) Mail Departure Agent
22. **What is the alignment of text that is positioned so that both the left and right edges of the paragraph are flush with the left and right margins?**
    (a) Centered (b) Justified
    (c) Right Aligned (d) Left Aligned
23. **Which of the following extensions are not related to LibreOffice?**
    (a) .ods (b) .odt
    (c) .rtf (d) .odp
24. **The speed of a dot matrix printer is measured in.**
    (a) Pages per second (b) Pages per minute
    (c) Characters per second
    (d) Character per minute
25. **If your computer is set up for for more than one user, you might need to ...., or select your user account name when the computer starts.**
    (a) Login (b) Restart
    (c) Shutdown (d) Logout
26. **Which is not a process of 3D printing?**
    (a) Power bed fusion (b) Programming
    (c) Material jetiing (d) None of the above
27. **Menu of Master Slide Function in LibreOffice Impress is:**
    (a) Slide (b) Slide Show
    (c) Tools (d) Format
28. **How many Row and Column are were is in Calc?**
    (a) 1024 & 1048576 (b) 1048576 & 1024
    (c) 16384 & 1048576 (d) 1048576 & 16384
29. **Which of the following is considered as first web browser?**
    (a) Internet Explorer (b) Nexus
    (c) Mosaic (d) Netscape Navigator
30. **Antivirus software protects against which of the following types of malware?**
    (a) Trojan Horses (b) Viruses
    (c) Worms (d) All of the above
31. **What is the minimum zoom size in LibreOffice Impress?**
    (a) 10% (b) 5%
    (c) 20% (d) 3000%
32. **Minimum age required to open saving account in the bank is:**
    (a) 10 years (b) 8 years
    (c) 12 years (d) None of the above
33. **What is a presentation in LibreOffice?**
    (a) Impress (b) Calc
    (c) Writer (d) None
34. **News groups are.....**
    (a) Discussion group (b) Chart service
    (c) E-mail service (d) None
35. **In which year was the first email sent?**
    (a) 1992 (b) 1982
    (c) 1971 (d) 1977
36. **In LibreOffice Calc functions being with the formula prefix ....**
    (a) = (b) @
    (c) + (d) #
37. **Which of the following is a valid email–**
    (a) sales@bpbonline.com
    (b) salesofbpb@online.com
    (c) sales.bpb.online@.com
    (d) @sales.bpbonline.com
38. **The first page that you normally view at a Web site is its.**
    (a) Master Page (b) Home Page
    (c) Banner (d) First Page
39. **The Internet uses:**
    (a) Packet Switching (b) Circuit Switching
    (c) Hybrid Switching (d) None of the above
40. **IIS refers to ....**
    (a) Internet Information Server
    (b) International Institute for Standards
    (c) Internal IP Scheme
    (d) Internet Information System
41. **What is meant by computer literacy?**
    (a) Ability to write computer programs
    (b) Knowing what a computer can and cannot do
    (c) Ability to assemble computers
    (d) Knowing computer related vocabulary

42. **The set of processed data is called?**
    (a) Data Processing (b) Data
    (c) Information (d) Database
43. **What is the hyperlink shortcut key in LibreOffice Writer?**
    (a) Ctrl+K (b) Ctrl+H
    (c) Ctrl+Shift+H (d) Ctrl+L
44. **Who is the present Governor of RBI?**
    (a) DK Mittal (b) KC Chakrabarty
    (c) Raghuram Rajan (d) Shaktikanta Das
45. **Which of the following is not a text function?**
    (a) VAR() (b) CHAR()
    (c) PMT() (d) LEN()
46. **LibreOffice Calc has a file extension?**
    (a) .ods (b) .doc
    (c) .xls (d) .odp
47. **What happens to the date and time shortcuts in LibreOffice Calc and Excel?**
    (a) Ctrl+Shift+: (b) Ctrl+;
    (c) Both (a) and (b) (d) None
48. **What will to the result from adding A1+A2 to Calc?**
    (a) 0 (b) ###
    (c) 1 (d) None of the above
49. **A specific page of web is known as ....**
    (a) Webpage (b) Text
    (c) Document (d) None of above
50. **What is the maximum number of worksheets in Calc?**
    (a) 1000 (b) 10000
    (c) 255 (d) 5000
51. **Capitalization is not at all necessary when writting email.**
    (a) True (b) False
52. **To clear all temporary files, we perform disk clean-up.**
    (a) True (b) False
53. **One millibyte is equivalent to 1000 byte.**
    (a) True (b) False
54. **LibreOffice has many software.**
    (a) True (b) False
55. **Star, Bus, Ring, Tree, Graph and Mesh are examples of network topologies.**
    (a) True (b) False
56. **NEFT stand for National Electronic Funds Transfer which is a system for electronic transfer of money from one bank to another.**
    (a) True (b) False
57. **A markup language such as HTML allows us to embed formatting instructions in the file itself.**
    (a) True (b) False
58. **AMD stands for Advanced Micro Devices.**
    (a) True (b) False
59. **A signature contains text that automatically appears at the bottom of each e-mail message you compose.**
    (a) True (b) False
60. **One of the advantages of a PC network is that the files can be shared.**
    (a) True (b) False
61. **Trojan Horses are very similar to virus in the matter that they are computer programs that replicate copies of themselves.**
    (a) True (b) False
62. **Mouse is an output devices.**
    (a) True (b) False
63. **Asynchronous Transmission Mode (ATM) circuits are appropriate circuit for transmission of voice and real-time data.**
    (a) True (b) False
64. **To set the contents of a cell in right alignment, Ctrl+R is used.**
    (a) True (b) False
65. **Clicking on a Icon with the mouse is a form of giving an instruction to the computer.**
    (a) True (b) False
66. **Is there a job Ctrl+F in LibreOffice that is in MS Office?**
    (a) True (b) False
67. **The Web is anoher name for the internet.**
    (a) True (b) False
68. **When posting to my groups wiki, it is okay for me to speak my mind, regardles of other group member's feelings.**
    (a) True (b) False
69. **A browser extension is a computer program that extends the functionally of a web browser.**
    (a) True (b) False
70. **To improve efficiency, servers normally store requested files in a cache in memory.**
    (a) True (b) False
71. **Filter is used to hide the unwanted data from worksheet.**
    (a) True (b) False

72. Once you have created a chart you may change everything about the chart.
(a) True (b) False
73. With a single bit you can represent any distinct items.
(a) True (b) False
74. Excel cannot insert multiple columns in its sheet.
(a) True (b) False
75. You can use e-mail to send message but not file across the internet.
(a) True (b) False
76. In Ms Excel 2013, we cannot insert multiple rows in its sheet.
(a) True (b) False
77. Is it possible to automatically forward all the incoming mail to another email address?
(a) True (b) False
78. Shift+Tab key is used to move to one cell down or to the next cell in sequence.
(a) True (b) False
79. Copying files from your computr to another computer on the internet is called file transferring.
(a) True (b) False
80. There are probably as many different reasons to publish a site on the Web as there are Web sites.
(a) True (b) False
81. Browsers are the programs that provide access to Web resources.
(a) True (b) False
82. A changed file can be closed without saving?
(a) True (b) False
83. A broadcast message is an example of simplex method.
(a) True (b) False
84. We cannot disable popups to appear in the browser.
(a) True (b) False
85. Movies & sounds inserted in a slide cannot be customised to play automatically; it can be played only manually at the presenter's request.
(a) True (b) False
86. The Back and Forward buttons can be used to visit only pages from the same website.
(a) True (b) False
87. Windows 10 taskbar sits at the bottom of the screen giving the user access to the Start Menu.
(a) True (b) False
88. TCP/IP defines an abstract interface through which hardware is addressed to hide the diversity of equipment that may be used in a networking environment.
(a) True (b) False
89. Primary name of a file can be used of 10 characters.
(a) True (b) False
90. Data in "TO" field of e-mail message window tells the email server where to send the email.
(a) True (b) False
91. Shortcut key of redo in LibreOffice is Ctrl+Y.
(a) True (b) False
92. To highlight the Para, double-click in the selection bar next to the paragraph.
(a) True (b) False
93. Two users using the same online mail service can have the same user name.
(a) True (b) False
94. In all IP addresses A, B and C the size of net id and host id are same.
(a) True (b) False
95. Algorithm and Flowchart help us to specify the problem completely and clearly.
(a) True (b) False
96. The Ctrl key is used with the mouse when you want to resize an image from the center and keep it proportioned.
(a) True (b) False
97. HDCL stands for High-Level Data Link Control.
(a) True (b) False
98. LibreOffice has the ability to close window by key Ctrl+W.
(a) True (b) False
99. Linux is a free open source operating system?
(a) True (b) False
100. Hacking a computer is always illegal and punishable by law.
(a) True (b) False

Answers

1.	(c)	2.	(b)	3.	(b)	4.	(d)
5.	(d)	6.	(b)	7.	(a)	8.	(c)
9.	(c)	10.	(d)	11.	(d)	12.	(a)
13.	(c)	14.	(b)	15.	(d)	16.	(c)
17.	(c)	18.	(b)	19.	(c)	20.	(b)
21.	(b)	22.	(b)	23.	(c)	24.	(c)

25.	(a)	26.	(b)	27.	(a)	28.	(b)
29.	(c)	30.	(d)	31.	(b)	32.	(a)
33.	(a)	34.	(a)	35.	(c)	36.	(a)
37.	(a)	38.	(b)	39.	(a)	40.	(a)
41.	(d)	42.	(c)	43.	(a)	44.	(d)
45.	(c)	46.	(a)	47.	(c)	48.	(a)
49.	(a)	50.	(b)	51.	(a)	52.	(a)
53.	(b)	54.	(a)	55.	(a)	56.	(a)
57.	(a)	58.	(a)	59.	(a)	60.	(a)
61	(b)	62.	(b)	63.	(a)	64.	(a)
65.	(a)	66.	(a)	67.	(a)	68.	(b)
69.	(a)	70.	(a)	71.	(a)	72.	(a)
73.	(b)	74.	(b)	75.	(f)	76.	(b)
77.	(a)	78.	(b)	79.	(b)	80.	(a)
81.	(a)	82.	(a)	83.	(a)	84.	(b)
85.	(b)	86.	(b)	87.	(a)	88.	(a)
89.	(b)	90.	(a)	91.	(a)	92.	(a)
93.	(b)	94.	(b)	95.	(a)	96.	(b)
97.	(a)	98.	(a)	99.	(a)	100.	(a)

Model Test Paper XXII

1. **Authentication is:**
   (a) Insertion
   (b) Hard to assure identity of user on a remote system
   (c) Modification
   (d) All of the above
2. **........ refers to the situation in which services or data become unavailable, unusable and destroyed.**
   (a) Interruption (b) Confidentiality
   (c) Integrity (d) All of the above
3. **In computer security, ... means that computer system assets can be modified only by authorised parties.**
   (a) Availability (b) Confidentiality
   (c) Integrity (d) All of the above
4. **In computer seurity, integrity refer to:**
   (a) Access to computer resources with difficul-ties
   (b) Viewing and printing of data
   (c) Separation and protection of the resources data
   (d) All of the above
5. **Which of the following provide protection?**
   (a) Data Access Controls
   (b) System Design
   (c) System Access Control
   (d) None of above
6. **In computer security, ... means that the information in a computer system can only be accessible to authorised parties.**
   (a) Integrity (b) Availability
   (c) Confidentiality (d) All of the above
7. **Encryption technique improve a network's ....**
   (a) Security (b) Performance
   (c) Reliability (d) None of these
8. **Which Protection method is used to monitor, who can access the data for what purpose?**
   (a) System Design
   (b) System Access Control
   (c) Data Access Control
   (d) None of above
9. **The main goals of secure computing is...**
   (a) Interruption (b) Confidentiality
   (c) Modification (d) All of the above
10. **.......... means that sender must not be able to deny sending a message that he sent.**
    (a) Integrity (b) Non-repudiation
    (c) Authentication (d) None of the above
11. **The Secure Electronic Transaction Protocol is used for which type of payment.......**
    (a) NEFT (b) Credit Card
    (c) Cheque (d) All of the above
12. **What are the three basic component of computer security?**
    (a) Control, intelligence, action
    (b) Confidentiality, integrity, availability
    (c) Confidence, integrity, action
    (d) Central, Intelligence, agency
13. **The aspect of security that fails, when an email in intercepted is:**
    (a) Privacy (b) Integrity
    (c) Authentication (d) All of the above
14. **For secure Electronic Data Interchange (EDI) transmission on internet use ....**
    (a) MIME (b) TCP/IP
    (c) S/MIME (d) None of above
15. **The creeper virus was eventually deleted by a program known as ....**
    (a) The reaper (b) The weaper
    (c) The seaper (d) None of above
16. **Which of the following means that the receiver is ensured that the massage is coming from the intended sender, not an imposter?**
    (a) Access Control (b) Availability
    (c) Authentication (d) All of the above
17. **Software programs that close potential security breaches in an operating systems are known as:**
    (a) Refresh patches (b) Security patches
    (c) Security breath fixes (d) All of the above
18. **........... means to prove/verify the identity of the entity that tries to access the system's resources.**
    (a) Password authentication
    (b) Message authentication
    (c) Entity authentication
    (d) All of the above

19. Malware is used to

(a) Gather sensitive information
(b) Disrupt computer operation
(c) Both (a) and (b)
(d) All of the above

20. A major security problem for operating system is

(a) Human problem
(b) Physical problem
(c) Authentication problem
(d) All of the above

21. .... is included in Internet of things.

(a) Sensors, actuator (b) Software
(c) WiFi technique (d) All of the above

22. Vision of the Industry 4.0 is:

(a) Internet of service (b) Internet of things
(c) Both (a) and (b) (d) None of the above

23. Included in Industry 4.0.

(a) Cloud computing (b) Internet of things
(c) Artificial intelligence
(d) All of the above

24. Unauthorised access is which type of network issue.

(a) Reliability (b) Security
(c) Performance (d) None of these

25. Firewall is a type of ....

(a) Virus (b) Output device
(c) threat (d) None of the above

26. Data security threats include

(a) Privacy invasion (b) Hardware failure
(c) Fraudulent manipulation of data
(d) All of the above

27. In SET protocol a customer sends a purchase order

(a) In a plain text form
(b) Using digitam signature system
(c) Encrypted with his public key
(d) None of above

28. Which of the following is/are threat(s) for electronic payment system?

(a) Trojan horse (b) Computer virus
(c) Computer worms (d) All of the above

29. Trend Micro is a ....

(a) Antivirus software (b) Program
(c) Virus program (d) All of the above

30. Which of the following is a class of computer threat:

(a) Stalking (b) Soliciting
(c) DoS attack (d) All of these

31. This is a type of SSL Certificate.

(a) Extended (b) WildCard
(c) Unified (d) All of the above

32. Benefits of Robotics process automation is?

(a) Enable employees productive
(b) Enable better customer service
(c) Processes to be complete more rapidly
(d) All of the above.

33. .... ensures that unauthorised users do not access the system.

(a) Data Access Control
(b) System Design
(c) System Access Control
(d) All of these

34. The certificate will be issued for both business and individuals use:

(a) Class 2 (b) Class 3
(c) Class 1 (d) All of above

35. ....is/are the branch of information technology which is intended to protect computer.

(a) IT security (b) Cyber security
(c) Information security (d) All of these

36. This is not a benfit of Big Data Analytics.

(a) Cost Reduction
(b) Faster, better decision making
(c) Manage of Data
(d) None of the above

37. Which is a Mobile Social Network?

(a) Instagram (b) Facebook
(c) Twitter (d) All of above

38. This is not a type of cyber attacks.

(a) Attacks on integrity
(b) Attacks on confidentality
(c) Attacks on property
(d) All of the above

39. Which is a benefit of Cloud Computing?

(a) Fast speed (b) Low cost
(c) More secure (d) All of the above

40. Include in Artificial Intelligence:

(a) Planning (b) Knowledge
(c) Both (a) and (b) (d) None of these

41. Which social media is more based on Image and Video.

(a) Instagram (b) Facebook
(c) Twitter (d) None of these

42. Which social media is more based on mobile compare desktop.
(a) Twitter (b) Facebook
(c) Instagram (d) None of these

43. What is a Smart Factory?
(a) Robots who will replace people
(b) Factories and logistic systems that will operate and organise themselves without human interaction
(c) Both (a) and (b)
(d) None of the above

44. Which industry branches are suitable for industry 4.0 development?
(a) Industry 4.0 is the first instance an enrichment for the service industry.
(b) Industries 4.0 can be used in all industrial contexts where processes need to be more intelligent.
(c) Especially in the automative and agricultural sector.
(d) None of the above.

45. Which of the following tools/applications relate to Industry 4.0.
(a) Performance Manager
(b) Condition Monitoring
(c) 3D visualization
(d) None of the above

46. .... design principles are applied for Industry 4.0.
(a) Two (b) Four
(c) Six (d) None of the above

47. The objective for industry 4.0 is ....
(a) Reduced complexity
(b) Increase efficiency
(c) Enabled self controlling
(d) All of above

48. IoT stand for......
(a) Industry of Things (b) Intranet of Things
(c) Internet of Things (d) None of the above

49. IIoT stands for:
(a) Internet of Things
(b) Industrial Internet of Things
(c) Interanet of Things
(d) None of these

50. Which of the followings option is not best described about Industry 4.0.
(a) Speed (b) Smart Factory
(c) Analytics (d) None of the above

51. Industry 4.0 is based on the basis of Development of Machines.
(a) True (b) False

52. The certificate authority signs the digital certificate with it's own Private key.
(a) True (b) False

53. Industry 4.0 is a new technology for politician.
(a) True (b) False

54. The main function of proxy application gateway firewall is to allow intranet users to securely use specified internet services.
(a) True (b) False

55. A firewall is a security device deployed at the boundary of a corporate intranet to protect it from the unathorised access.
(a) True (b) False

56. A firewall may be implemented in routers which connect intranet to internet.
(a) True (b) False

57. When a server goes down, this is a network reliability issue.
(a) True (b) False

58. Firewall is a program of hardware that filters the information coming through an internet connection or computer system.
(a) True (b) False

59. A virus is a network security issue.
(a) True (b) False

60. Spyware monitors user activity on internet and transmit that information in the background to someone else.
(a) True (b) False

61. Companies providing cloud services enable users to store files and applications on remote servers, and then access all the data via the internet.
(a) True (b) False

62. Example of social network are Facebook, Twitter etc.
(a) True (b) False

63. The objective of Industry 4.0 is to increase the efficiency.
(a) True (b) False

64. Instagram is a mobile social media owned by google.
(a) True (b) False

65. Linkedin is the largest mobile social network.
(a) True (b) False

66. In the smart factory workers, machines and resources communicate easily.

(a) True (b) False

67. Fishing is a form of fraud where fraudulent emails are sent from reputable sources.
(a) True (b) False

68. Sophisticated software programs are used for Big Data Analytics.
(a) True (b) False

69. If s' is missing in the URL means that site is secure.
(a) True (b) False

70. The step Data-Information-Knowledge-Western-Decision. Turn big data become smart data.
(a) True (b) False

71. Robotics Process Automation (RPA) is a part of an organization's IT infrastructure.
(a) True (b) False

72. Robotics is also a major field related to Artificial intelligence.
(a) True (b) False

73. Software is a service of Platform for creating software.
(a) True (b) False

74. Data may be collected from social network, digital image, sensor and sales transaction.
(a) True (b) False

75. Virtual Reality and augmented Reality are two sides of the same coin.
(a) True (b) False

76. Microsoft Azure is an example of public cloud.
(a) True (b) False

77. Amazon Elastic is an example of private cloud.
(a) True (b) False

78. The Internet of things allows to interact and exchange data with devices.
(a) True (b) False

79. The way of Industry 4.0 leads to the connectivity of virtual world and physical objects.
(a) True (b) False

80. In the internet of things, information system can not be access remotely.
(a) True (b) False

81. Firewall is a type of threat.
(a) True (b) False

82. Six design principals are applied for Industry 4.0.
(a) True (b) False

83. Digital signature develop two types of key one private key and second public key that all linked mathematically .
(a) True (b) False

84. Facebook and Instagram is a mobile social network?
(a) True (b) False

85. Phishing is the type of cyber security?
(a) True (b) False

86. Blockchain was invented by a person using the name Satoshi Nakamoto in 2008 to serve as the public transaction ledger of the cryptocurrency bitoin.
(a) True (b) False

87. Cyber security protects the data and integrity of computing assets belonging to or connecting to an organization's network.
(a) True (b) False

88. Oculus Rift, Oculus VR and Facebook are the major players in Virtual Reality.
(a) True (b) False

89. Phone security is the practice of defending mobile devices against a wide range of cyber attack.
(a) True (b) False

90. Attacks on confidentiality is not a type of cyber attack.
(a) True (b) False

91. Back up your files regularly to prevent cyber security attacks.
(a) True (b) False

92. A typical enterprise uses multiple and disconnected IT systems to run its operations.
(a) True (b) False

93. Big online business website like Flipkart, Snapdeal uses Facebook or Gmail data to view the customer information or behavior.
(a) True (b) False

94. A blockchain carries no transaction cost.
(a) True (b) False

95. Cloud Computing offers online development and deployment tools, programming runtime environment.
(a) True (b) False

96. Attacks on integrity is the type of cyber security.
(a) True (b) False

97. Computer Viruses are man made.
(a) True (b) False

98. Low cost and Fast speed is a benefit of cloud Computing?
(a) True (b) False

99. Instagram social media is more based on mobile computing man desktop.

(a) True (b) False

100. Trend micro is a program.

(a) True (b) False

Answers

1.	(b)	2.	(a)	3.	(c)	4.	(c)
5.	(b)	6.	(c)	7.	(a)	8.	(a)
9.	(b)	10.	(b)	11.	(b)	12.	(b)
13.	(d)	14.	(c)	15.	(a)	16.	(c)
17.	(b)	18.	(c)	19.	(c)	20.	(c)
21.	(b)	22.	(c)	23.	(d)	24.	(b)
25.	(d)	26.	(a)	27.	(b)	28.	(d)
29.	(a)	30.	(c)	31.	(b)	32.	(d)
33.	(c)	34.	(a)	35.	(d)	36.	(c)
37.	(d)	38.	(c)	39.	(d)	40.	(c)
41.	(a)	42.	(c)	43.	(b)	44.	(b)
45.	(a)	46.	(c)	47.	(d)	48.	(c)
49.	(b)	50.	(a)	51.	(b)	52.	(a)
53.	(b)	54.	(a)	55.	(a)	56.	(a)
57.	(a)	58.	(a)	59.	(a)	60.	(a)
61	(a)	62.	(a)	63.	(a)	64.	(b)
65.	(b)	66.	(a)	67.	(a)	68.	(a)
69.	(b)	70.	(a)	71.	(b)	72.	(a)
73.	(b)	74.	(a)	75.	(a)	76.	(a)
77.	(b)	78.	(a)	79.	(a)	80.	(b)
81.	(a)	82.	(a)	83.	(a)	84.	(b)
85.	(a)	86.	(a)	87.	(a)	88.	(a)
89.	(a)	90.	(b)	91.	(a)	92.	(a)
93.	(a)	94.	(a)	95.	(a)	96.	(a)
97.	(a)	98.	(a)	99.	(a)	100.	(a)

Model Test Paper XXIII

1. **In which year NEFT services has been started:**
   (a) 2002 (b) 2005
   (c) 2006 (d) 2001
2. **The Indian rupee symbol '₹' officially adopted in:**
   (a) 2010 (b) 2009
   (c) 2015 (d) 2012
3. **Interest on savings deposit is paid:**
   (a) Every month (b) Yearly
   (c) Quarterly (d) Half yearly
4. **Under PMSBY, accidental death claim is available for:**
   (a) Rs. 2 lac (b) Rs. 1 lac
   (c) Rs. 3 lac (d) None of above
5. **QR code stand for:**
   (a) Quick Result Code
   (b) Quick Response Code
   (c) Quick Restore Code
   (d) None of above
6. **ATM means:**
   (a) Auto Truck of Mahindra
   (b) Any Time Money
   (c) Automated Teller Machine
   (d) None of the above
7. **KYC means:**
   (a) Know your character
   (b) Know your customer
   (c) Both (a) and (b)
   (d) None of the above
8. **Which of the following is type of credit card.**
   (a) Visa (b) Master
   (c) Both (a) and (b) (d) None of these
9. **Which of the following is known as online banking?**
   (a) Internet banking (b) Net banking
   (c) Both (a) and (b) (d) None of above
10. **Can illiterate person be issued Debit card?**
    (a) Yes (b) No
    (c) Only in case he is head of family
    (d) Only in case of joint account
11. **UPI payment interface is developed by......**
    (a) Finance Ministry
    (b) National Payment Corporation
    (c) Bank (d) None of the above
12. **Pradhan Mantri Suraksha Bima Yojna (PMSBY) was launched on:**
    (a) April 9, 2015 (b) May 9, 2015
    (c) May 1, 2015 (d) May 20, 2015
13. **In Pradhan Mantri Mudra Yojana, under the SHI-SHU category loan amount is:**
    (a) Up to 50000 (b) Up to 30000
    (c) Up to 10000 (d) Up to 90000
14. **Which type of deposits earns higher interest rate?**
    (a) Fixed Deposit
    (b) Current Account
    (c) Saving Accounts
    (d) None of the above
15. **The amount of money to be charged for a certain amount of insurane coverage is called?**
    (a) Premium (b) Token Money
    (c) Insured Money (d) Cash
16. **Main security of internet banking is:**
    (a) User name (b) Password
    (c) User mobile number (d) User address
17. **Through .... App you can transfer the money but cannot do any payment as bill/shopping.**
    (a) PAYTM (b) BHIM
    (c) Both (a) and (b) (d) None of these
18. **Atal Pension Yojna is open to Indian citizens whose age are between:**
    (a) 25–40 (b) 18–40
    (c) 18–25 (d) 25–18
19. **Which mobile wallet does not permit cash withdrawal:**
    (a) Semi Open Wallet (b) Open Wallet
    (c) Semi Closed Wallet (d) None of the above
20. **In case of a cancellation or return of the order which mobile wallets are used by compnies:**
    (a) Semi Open Wallet (b) Open Wallet
    (c) Closed Walled (d) None of these
21. **Bank does not give loan against:**
    (a) LIC Policy (b) Gold Ornaments
    (c) NSC (d) Lottery Ticket
22. **Ful form of DFT is:**

(a) Digital Financial Tools
(b) Dynamic Financial Tools
(c) Double Finance Tools
(d) Digital Fund Tools

23. **Bank pay interest on:**
(a) Deposits (b) Loans
(c) Both (a) and (b) (d) None of the options

24. **Account payee cheques can be paid:**
(a) At ATM
(b) At cash counter of bank
(c) By deposit in bank account
(d) None of the above

25. **What is the validity period of cheque?**
(a) 3 months from date of issue
(b) 4 months from date of issue
(c) Unlimited
(d) 1 month from date of issue

26. **A valid email address is.**
(a) @sales@bpbonline.com
(b) sales@bpbonline.com
(c) sales@bpbonline.on
(d) sales.bpbonline.com

27. **Which of the following is not an email server.**
(a) Outlook (b) Rediff mail
(c) Both (a) and (b) (d) Linkden

28. **Which of the following protocols is used by internet mail?**
(a) TCP/IP (b) HTTP
(c) FTP (d) None of these

29. **With the email we can attach:**
(a) Not more than two files
(b) Not more than one file
(c) One file (d) None of these

30. **In which year was the first email sent?**
(a) 1992 (b) 1982
(c) 1971 (d) 1977

31. **IRC stands for:**
(a) Internet Routing Channel
(b) Internet Resource Channel
(c) Internet Relay Chet
(d) Internet Rights Council

32. **E-mail message can be protected by**
(a) Caching (b) Mirroring
(c) Resending (d) Encryption

33. **Messenger Mailbox is present in ......**
(a) Netscape Communicator
(b) Internet Explorer
(c) Both (a) and (b) (d) None of the above

34. **Which of these should be avoided in an E-mail?**
(a) Subject line
(b) Wrong email address
(c) Re-reading (d) Smileys

35. **A smile protocol used for fetching on e-mail from a mailbox is ......**
(a) POP3 (b) POP2
(c) IMAP (d) None

36. **Smile us present by the following emotion display.**
(a) Laughing face (b) Confused face
(c) Amazed face (d) Shocked face

37. **Shortkey face is presenting to which of the following emotion display**
(a) Laughing face (b) Confused face
(c) Sad face (d) Amazed face

38. **The conveninent place to store contact information for quick retrieval is:**
(a) Message box (b) Addres box
(c) Address book (d) None of these

39. **The email component of Internet Explorer is called:**
(a) Outlook Express (b) Message Box
(c) Messenger Mailbox (d) None of the above

40. **The domain name in an URL is refers to:**
(a) Server (b) Protocol
(c) Directory (d) Filename

41. **The internet standard is:**
(a) Bin Hex (b) MIME
(c) None26 (d) Unencoding

42. **Email address is made up of an:**
(a) In second part (b) In first part
(c) In third part (d) None of these

43. **MIME stands for:**
(a) Multiple internet mail extension
(b) Multipurpose internet mail extension
(c) Multiple International mail extension
(d) None of these

44. **In email address, the symbol that is used to separate the user name with he ISP address is .....**
(a) & (b) #
(c) % (d) @

45. If an email is received by an unknown person then
(a) One should open it and respond saying you don't know them
(b) One should open it and respond asking their personal information
(c) It should be forwarded to police
(d) It should be deleted without opening it

46. What is the term used for talking on Internet with the help of typed text?
(a) Email (b) New group
(c) Chatting (d) None of these

47. .... indicates copies of the message were sent to additional people and the recipient does not know the message has been sent to others.
(a) Cc (b) URL
(c) Bcc (d) End

48. SMTP is associated with:
(a) Electronic Mail (b) TCP/IP
(c) WWW (d) Internet Explorer

49. Which of these is the easiest way of communication?
(a) Telephone (b) Email
(c) Letter (d) Fax

50. Which of these do not provide free Emal?
(a) Rediff (b) Hotmail
(c) Yahoo (d) WhatsApp

51. You can not withdraw cash from Micro ATM.
(a) True (b) False

52. Bank Mitra works only in the areas where there is not ATMs and branches of banks.
(a) True (b) False

53. You can do online shopping recharge and bill payment through mobile wallet.
(a) True (b) False

54. Aadhar is a 12 digit number card & identity proof issued by Unique Indentification Authority of India (UIDAI).
(a) True (b) False

55. Personal loan can also be taken by private companies.
(a) True (b) False

56. For our daily savings, we use current account scheme.
(a) True (b) False

57. NPCI stand for National Payment Corporation of India.
(a) True (b) False

58. IFSC is an eleven digit code which is mandatory for transfer of fund through NEFT & RTGS.
(a) True (b) False

59. RBI means Reserve Bank of India defines the banking rules in India.
(a) True (b) False

60. AEPS stand for Aadhar Enabled Payment System.
(a) True (b) False

61. UPI mean Unified Payment Interface used to transfer payment at any time.
(a) True (b) False

62. Credit/Debit card is a type of plastic card issued by bank or any financial institution.
(a) True (b) False

63. ID proof and address proof documents required for opening an account in banks:
(a) True (b) False

64. NRI means Non Resident Indian.
(a) True (b) False

65. Bank provides gold loan only when gold are martgage in the bank as security:
(a) True (b) False

66. USSD means Unstructured Supplementary Service Data which allows users without a smartphone or Internet connection to use mobile banking through the *99#.
(a) True (b) False

67. RTGS means Real Time Gross Settlement is a fund transfer system used to transfer money from one bank to any other bank.
(a) True (b) False

68. POS means Point of Sale is an electronic machine used for paying on retail shop.
(a) True (b) False

69. APY provide monthly pension to subscribers from 50 years of age.
(a) True (b) False

70. In PMSBY, you can not claim for partial disability.
(a) True (b) False

71. IMPS stand for Immediate Payment Service.
(a) True (b) False

72. UPI stand for Unified Payments Interface.
(a) True (b) False

73. Mobile banking is a financial service facility for a customer to carry out financial transaction.
(a) True (b) False

74. TDS means Tax Deducted at Source.
(a) True (b) False

75. BHIM means Bharat Interface for Money, is an app launched by Pradhan Mantri on 30 December 2016 for transaction of money.
(a) True (b) False

76. IRC stands for Internet Relay Chat.
(a) True (b) False

77. MDA stands for Mail Delivery Agent.
(a) True (b) False

78. CC in the mail stands for Carbon Copy.
(a) True (b) False

79. To read an Email, you need to Sign In, with the Email Service.
(a) True (b) False

80. Email is a method of exchanging digital messages usually over Internet or network.
(a) True (b) False

81. Yahoo messenger is the chatting application.
(a) True (b) False

82. ICMP protocol is used to report error message.
(a) True (b) False

83. Web traffic on Internet is transferred by using FTP.
(a) True (b) False

84. The network address is usually encoded as a prefix of the IP address.
(a) True (b) False

85. WiFi can be used for connecting two machines without any cable.
(a) True (b) False

86. DigiLocker is a service launched by Government of India in February 2015 to provide a secure dedicated personal electronic space for storing the documents of residents Indian citizens.
(a) True (b) False

87. SMTP uses port 25, but SSL/TLS encrypted SMTP uses port 465.
(a) True (b) False

88. POP uses port 110, but SSL/TLS encrypted IMAP uses port 005.
(a) True (b) False

89. IMAP uses port 143, but SSL/TLS encrypted IMAP uses port 993.
(a) True (b) False

90. Usenet is a provider of news?
(a) True (b) False

91. The email address only requires user name.
(a) True (b) False

92. Bounced emails always result in messages being sent back to the sender.
(a) True (b) False

93. The two parts of an e-mail address is separated by @ symbol.
(a) True (b) False

94. Email can be used to send broadcast messages, but only within your own company.
(a) True (b) False

95. Email is limited to text besed messages.
(a) True (b) False

96. Email addresses are case-sensitive.
(a) True (b) False

97. You can use e-mail to send messages but not file across the Internet.
(a) True (b) False

98. In an email message, users in Cc fields cannot see other recipients whereas users in Bcc fields can see all the recipients of the message.
(a) True (b) False

99. A Meta Search engine maintains its own database information.
(a) True (b) False

100. The FTP protocol is the client/server program used to retrieve the document.
(a) True (b) False

Answers

1.	(b)	2.	(a)	3.	(d)	4.	(a)
5.	(b)	6.	(c)	7.	(b)	8.	(c)
9.	(c)	10.	(a)	11.	(b)	12.	(b)
13.	(a)	14.	(a)	15.	(a)	16.	(b)
17.	(c)	18.	(b)	19.	(a)	20.	(c)
21.	(d)	22.	(a)	23.	(a)	24.	(c)
25.	(a)	26.	(c)	27.	(d)	28.	(d)
29.	(d)	30.	(c)	31.	(c)	32.	(d)
33.	(a)	34.	(b)	35.	(a)	36.	(a)
37.	(d)	38.	(c)	39.	(a)	40.	(a)
41.	(b)	42.	(a)	43.	(b)	44.	(d)
45.	(d)	46.	(c)	47.	(a)	48.	(a)
49.	(b)	50.	(d)	51.	(b)	52.	(a)
53.	(a)	54.	(a)	55.	(b)	56.	(b)
57.	(a)	58.	(a)	59.	(a)	60.	(a)

61	(a)	62.	(a)	63.	(a)	64.	(a)	81.	(b)	82.	(a)	83.	(b)	84.	(a)
65.	(a)	66.	(a)	67.	(a)	68.	(a)	85.	(a)	86.	(a)	87.	(a)	88.	(a)
69.	(b)	70.	(b)	71.	(a)	72.	(a)	89.	(a)	90.	(a)	91.	(b)	92.	(a)
73.	(b)	74.	(a)	75.	(a)	76.	(a)	93.	(a)	94.	(b)	95.	(b)	96.	(b)
77.	(a)	78.	(a)	79.	(a)	80.	(a)	97.	(b)	98.	(b)	99.	(b)	100.	(a)

Model Test Paper XXIV

1. **The Internet uses:**
   (a) Packet Switching (b) Circuit Switching
   (c) Hybrid Switching (d) None of the above
2. **Which of the following is considered as first web browser?**
   (a) Internet Explorer (b) Nexus
   (c) Mosaic (d) Netscape Navigator
3. **A specific page of web is known as:**
   (a) Document (b) Worksheet
   (c) Webpage (d) None of above
4. **Software which allows user to view the webpage is called as:**
   (a) Interpreter (b) Website
   (c) Operating System (d) Internet Browser
5. **Unserved Ticketing System (UTS) through App is launched by Railway Ministry in:**
   (a) February 2019 (b) January 2019
   (c) January 2018 (d) None of the above
6. **Which of the following is a Web browsing software:**
   (a) Mozila Firefox (b) Google Chrome
   (c) Apple Safarid (d) All of the above
7. **Web page can be developed by using language:**
   (a) WWW (b) HTML
   (c) Internet Explorer (d) Web Browser
8. **The World Wide Web is composed of**
   (a) Only 100 pages (b) 1 page
   (c) Millions of Web pages
   (d) 500 Web pages
9. **WAIS stands for:**
   (a) Wide Area Internet Service
   (b) Wide Area Information Servers
   (c) Wide Area Information System
   (d) None of the above
10. **The internet was originally developed by ....**
    (a) Computer hackers
    (b) A corporation
    (c) The University of Michigan
    (d) U.S. Department of Defence
11. **A host on the Internet finds another host by its:**
    (a) Electronic address
    (b) Postal address
    (c) IP address
    (d) None of these
12. **A client program used to access the Internet services and resources available through the World Wide Web.**
    (a) Web Browser (b) ISP
    (c) Web Server (d) None of these
13. **Internet .... is:**
    (a) Network of Network
    (b) Operating System
    (c) Interpretor (d) Server
14. **Each computer connected to the internet is called is:**
    (a) Search Engine (b) Client/Server
    (c) Web Browser (d) None of the above
15. **Web first page of website is known as the:**
    (a) Home page (b) Main page
    (c) Both (a) and (b) (d) None of the above
16. **Who was the father of Internet?**
    (a) Vint Cerf (b) Chares Babbage
    (c) Martin Cooper (d) Denis Riche
17. **The communication protocol used by Internet is:**
    (a) Telnet (b) HTTP
    (c) TCP/IP (d) UTP
18. **.............. is used to save file in LibreOffice**
    (a) Ctrl+A (b) Ctrl+S
    (c) Ctrl+V (d) Ctrl+X
19. **ISP stands for:**
    (a) International Service Provider
    (b) Internal Service Provider
    (c) Intranet Service Provider
    (d) Internet Service Provider
20. **Internet is:**
    (a) Decentralized System
    (b) Complex System
    (c) Dianomic System
    (d) All of above
21. **........ are the two more widely used protocol for LANs.**
    (a) ASP/IP and TCP/IP
    (b) TCP/IP and Ethernet
    (c) Ethernet and Token Ring
    (d) Token Ring and ASP/IP

22. The following is NOT an Internet search engine.
(a) Crawler (b) Google
(c) Scientia ans (d) Excite

23. IP stand for:
(a) Internet Priority Protocol
(b) Internet Mass Protocol
(c) Internet Property Protocol
(d) Internet Protocol

24. Which of the following is related to internet security?
(a) CERT (b) W3C
(c) DSL (d) MIT

25. Internet Explorer is a type of:
(a) Compiler (b) Operating System
(c) Browser (d) IP Address

26. Which of the following devices can be used to input printed text:
(a) OMR (b) OCR
(c) MICR (d) All of the above

27. Which type of storage device is a BIOS?
(a) Secondary (b) Primary
(c) Teritiary (d) Not a storage device

28. Hard disk is coated in both side by:
(a) Optical Metalic Oxide
(b) Magnatic Metalic Oxide
(c) Carbon Layer
(d) All of the above

29. Which of the following are latest IT Gadgets
(a) Drone Camera (b) Pen with camera
(c) Both (a) and (b) (d) None of the above

30. A floppy disk contains
(a) Sectors only (b) Circular tracks only
(c) Both (a) and (b) (d) None of the above

31. The output devices make it possible for:
(a) Storage of Data
(b) Look and Print of Data
(c) Input of Data
(d) None of these

32. ..... is the high speed memory used in the computer.
(a) BIOS (b) RAM
(c) Cache (d) Hard Disk

33. USB is which type of storage device?
(a) Secondary (b) Primary
(c) Tertiary (d) None of these

34. When a computer prints a report, this output is called:
(a) Soft Copy (b) Hard Copy
(c) Harsh Copy (d) None of the above

35. The most common input device used today is the:
(a) CPU (b) Motherboard
(c) System Unit (d) Keyboard

36. Which component of computer is consider as its Heart?
(a) Keyboard (b) Monitor
(c) Microprocessor (d) Scanner

37. The Recyle Bin is configured automatically to be able to store files equal to .... of the size of your hard disk.
(a) 10 percent (b) 15 percent
(c) 1 percent (d) 5 percent

38. Which of the following memories allows simultaneous read and writes operations?
(a) RAM (b) ROM
(c) EPROM (d) None

39. .... is the result produce by a computer.
(a) Memory (b) Data
(c) Input (d) Output

40. The most common pointing input device is:
(a) Touch Pad (b) Track Ball
(c) Mouse (d) Touch Screen

41. What is the name of first super computer of India?
(a) PARAM 8000 (b) Saga 220
(c) PARAM 6000 (d) ENIAC

42. .... has a limitation that we can only add information to it but cannot or modify it.
(a) Floppy Drive (b) Tape Drive
(c) Hard Disk (d) CD Rom

43. Which of the following memories has the shortest access times?
(a) Magnetic Bubble Memory
(b) Cache Memory
(c) Ram
(d) Magnetic Core memory

44. Which one of these stores more data than a DVD?
(a) Floppy (b) CD Rom
(c) Red Ray Disk (d) Blue Ray Disk

45. DVD is based on:
(a) Magnetic Disk Technology
(b) USB Pen technology
(c) Optical Disk Technology

(d) Media to store Video data only

46. Which of the following is the largest unit of storage?

(a) TB (b) MB

(c) KB (d) GB

47. Which of the following is used for calculation work.

(a) Mouse (b) CU

(c) CPU (d) ALU

48. Which of the following is an output device?

(a) Scanner (b) Plotter

(c) Light Pen (d) Joystick

49. The set of processed data is called?

(a) Data Processing (b) Data

(c) Information (d) Database

50. In computer terminology, information means

(a) Important and Understandable Data

(b) Only Data

(c) Program

(d) Alphanumeric Data

51. The Internet is a collection of files.

(a) True (b) False

52. Wi-Fi stands for Wireless Fidelity.

(a) True (b) False

53. A hotspot is a physical location where people may obtain Internet access, typically by using Wi-Fi technology.

(a) True (b) False

54. The favourite features of Internet Explorer allows you to save the URLs of Web pages you visit frequently.

(a) True (b) False

55. The Web is another name for the internet.

(a) True (b) False

56. Copying files from your computer to another computer on the internet is called uploading.

(a) True (b) False

57. IMAP stands for Internet Message Access Protocol.

(a) True (b) False

58. IETF stands for Internet Engineering Task Force.

(a) True (b) False

59. Internet is a network of compuers linking many different types of computers all over the world.

(a) True (b) False

60. The Uniform Resource Locator (URL) is a standard for specifying any kind of information on the internet.

(a) True (b) False

61. The equipment needed to allow most home computers to connect to the internet is called a peripheral.

(a) True (b) False

62. The internet is a metropolitan area network (MAN).

(a) True (b) False

63. Dial-up and WiFi is a type of internet modem.

(a) True (b) False

64. ISP means Internet Service Provider is a company that provides an Internet connection

(a) True (b) False

65. A set of rules is known as protocol.

(a) True (b) False

66. FTP means File Transfer Protocol servers store files that you can transfer to or from your computer if you have on FTP client.

(a) True (b) False

67. Using LAN you can connect various computers in a building.

(a) True (b) False

68. HTML is used for creating home page for World Wide Web.

(a) True (b) False

69. Internet is a company's internal web.

(a) True (b) False

70. Extranet is a web within a web.

(a) True (b) False

71. Wide Area Information Servers or WAIS is a client-server text searching system.

(a) True (b) False

72. Google earth can be used for viewing satellite image, maps and other location on earth.

(a) True (b) False

73. Cookies stores information about the web pages in your favorites list.

(a) True (b) False

74. Hiring leased lines is cheaper than a dial-up connection on the Internet.

(a) True (b) False

75. HTML is similar to search engine.

(a) True (b) False

76. A mouse comes with exactly three buttons.

(a) True (b) False

77. System bus is used to connect CPU to a central switch.

(a) True (b) False

78. To improve efficiency, servers normally store requested files in a cache in memory.
(a) True (b) False

79. With a single bit you can represent any two distinct items.
(a) True (b) False

80. 1Kbit is 1024 bytes.
(a) True (b) False

81. The text editor is used to create, modifiy, and store a text file.
(a) True (b) False

82. Ram Memory is non volatile memory.
(a) True (b) False

83. VDUs can be used both as an input and output devices.
(a) True (b) False

84. The decimal equivalent of $(1101011)_2$ be 107.
(a) True (b) False

85. If a memory chip can store 100 KB, it can hold approximately 100,000 bytes:
(a) True (b) False

86. An application receiving data is called client Application.
(a) True (b) False

87. ALU is a part of CPU.
(a) True (b) False

88. Primary memory has higher storage capacity than secondary memory.
(a) True (b) False

89. ALU contains CPU, memory boards, device boards, power plugs, etc."
(a) True (b) False

90. A system can have more than one web browser installed at the same time.
(a) True (b) False

91. Before disk can be used to store data. It must be formatted.
(a) True (b) False

92. A cookie can execute code on your computer.
(a) True (b) False

93. Several windows can be opened at one time.
(a) True (b) False

94. Hard disk can have more than two heads.
(a) True (b) False

95. We can access data randomly which is stored on magnetic tape.
(a) True (b) False

96. ALU is used to store data.
(a) True (b) False

97. We can navigate all pages in Print Preview?
(a) True (b) False

98. Smart Watch 360, google glass, and drone camera are the example of latest IT Gadgets.
(a) True (b) False

99. Information is carried in data communication thousands of kilometres.
(a) True (b) False

100. A utility program is a type of system software that is used to perform a specific task to solve the common problems of software and hardware.
(a) True (b) False

Answers

1.	(a)	2.	(b)	3.	(c)	4.	(d)
5.	(d)	6.	(d)	7.	(b)	8.	(b)
9.	(b)	10.	(d)	11.	(d)	12.	(a)
13.	(d)	14.	(b)	15.	(a)	16.	(a)
17.	(c)	18.	(b)	19.	(d)	20.	(c)
21.	(c)	22.	(c)	23.	(d)	24.	(a)
25.	(c)	26.	(b)	27.	(b)	28.	(b)
29.	(c)	30.	(c)	31.	(b)	32.	(c)
33.	(c)	34.	(b)	35.	(d)	36.	(c)
37.	(d)	38.	(a)	39.	(d)	40.	(c)
41.	(a)	42.	(d)	43.	(b)	44.	(d)
45.	(c)	46.	(a)	47.	(d)	48.	(b)
49.	(c)	50.	(a)	51.	(b)	52.	(a)
53.	(a)	54.	(a)	55.	(a)	56.	(a)
57.	(a)	58.	(a)	59.	(a)	60.	(a)
61	(a)	62.	(b)	63.	(a)	64.	(a)
65.	(a)	66.	(a)	67.	(a)	68.	(a)
69.	(a)	70.	(a)	71.	(a)	72.	(a)
73.	(a)	74.	(b)	75.	(b)	76.	(a)
77.	(a)	78.	(a)	79.	(b)	80.	(a)
81.	(a)	82.	(b)	83.	(a)	84.	(a)
85.	(a)	86.	(a)	87.	(a)	88.	(b)
89.	(b)	90.	(a)	91.	(a)	92.	(b)
93.	(a)	94.	(a)	95.	(b)	96.	(b)
97.	(a)	98.	(a)	99.	(a)	100.	(a)

www.ingramcontent.com/pod-product-compliance
Ingram Content Group UK Ltd.
Pitfield, Milton Keynes, MK11 3LW, UK
UKHW061828190726
13853UKWH00009B/2495

9 789389 845242